T0293091

Authentic Customer Centricity

A Journey Towards Sustainable Customer Experience

Authentic Customer Centricity

A Journey Towards Sustainable
Customer Experience

Alkhatani Saad Zafer

INFORMATION AGE PUBLISHING, INC.
Charlotte, NC • www.infoagepub.com

Library of Congress Cataloging-in-Publication Data

A CIP record for this book is available from the Library of Congress
http://www.loc.gov

ISBN: 978-1-62396-912-7 (Paperback)
         978-1-62396-913-4 (Hardcover)
         978-1-62396-914-1 (ebook)

Copyright © 2015 Information Age Publishing Inc.

All rights reserved. No part of this publication may be reproduced, stored in a
retrieval system, or transmitted, in any form or by any means, electronic, mechanical,
photocopying, microfilming, recording or otherwise, without written permission
from the publisher.

Printed in the United States of America

Contents

Foreword

Hubert Rampersad

Customers are critical for the success of a firm and the most valuable asset. As Peter Drucker said "it is the customer who determines what a business is, what it produces and whether it will prosper." Becoming a customer centric company that focuses on the alignment of people, processes and technology that support a customer centric strategy is therefore needed to be capable of providing the right customer experience at the right time. This will result in high customer relations and increase in customer loyalty. It is a key source of competitive differentiation in the constantly evolving markets.

In this book, Dr. Zafer has provided a sorely needed guidebook for executives to become a successful customer centric company. He shows us how companies can deliver a superior customer experience that result in trusted customer relations that can boost profitability. This is the book you should read if you want to deliver a superior customer experience in a sustainable way.

Professor Hubert Rampersad, Ph.D. is President at Technological University of the Americas in Silicon Valley, California, USA (info@tua.university | www.tua.university) and author of Harvard Business School endorsed books *Authentic Personal Branding,*

Authentic Customer Centricity, pages vii–viii
Copyright © 2015 by Information Age Publishing
All rights of reproduction in any form reserved.

Personal Balanced Scorecard, Total Performance Scorecard, TPS-Lean Six Sigma, Authentic Governance, Authentic Personal Brand Coaching, and *Entrepreneurial Leadership Brand Coaching for Sustainable High Performance.* He is a former MIT Sloan guest professor.

Foreword

Ramazan Demir

We are living in a fast pace knowledge-economy. With the advances of communications industry of social internet and of data processing capabilities customers are more and more in a position to disrupt business value-chains. Customer centricity will continue to push organizations think along customer lifecycle and value proposition. So, customer centricity will continue to be a central them for businesses to ensure sustainable and profitable growth.

Dr. Saad's book highlights all critical aspects of a framework for organizations to graduate into a customer centric organization for excellence and sustainability. It is an authentic recipe and an effective feedback cycle for learning organizations. It also uniquely highlights differences between product centric organization and capabilities. Importantly, this book provides a real world application arising in a call center operations where customer experience is key for success.

Ramazan Demir, Ph.D. held leadership positions in marketplace products at Yahoo! in the USA, functioned as a board advisory for one of the largest advertising companies with operations in the USA and Europe, and recently functioned as the chief strategy and business development of a large telecommunications company. Dr. Demir holds a Ph.D. from MIT Sloan with five approved patents on Internet technology and products.

Authentic Customer Centricity, page ix
Copyright © 2015 by Information Age Publishing
All rights of reproduction in any form reserved.

Preface

Customer centricity is a vital ingredient for sustainability of organizations in today's digitally enabled globally connected world. At the core, customer centricity is about the delivery of organization's brand constituents to customers in the most differentiated and value generating ways. Organizations who can end-to-end oversee the value chain of customers and who can address customer experience touch points in a one-to-one mode will have the winning recipe for sustainable corporate development.

Organizations need to create learning feedback mechanisms to constantly better customer value chain economics and experience. Superior customer experience is the new constant for winning in the race. Companies can no longer rely on the traditional means of competitive differentiation. More information about the customer needs and expectations are becoming more vital for their success, understanding needs and requirements of end users is vital while having a good vantage point of product marketplace is critical. Organizations needs to constantly revamp their operating models to support customer centricity. Human capital is becoming more differentiator towards this quest. In this book I introduce an authentic customer centricity model that will support you to create a sustainable customer centric organization which enables organizations to effectively address right customer with the right value proposition and treatment at the right time. I would like to express my thanks to Dr. Hubert Rampersad, Dr. Ramazan Demir, and Dr. Rudy Garrity, who have given constructive

Authentic Customer Centricity, pages xi–xii
Copyright © 2015 by Information Age Publishing
All rights of reproduction in any form reserved.

feedback and encouragement. The authentic customer centricity model, described in this book, has been derived from Dr. Rampersad's Authentic Branding model (Rampersad, 2008, 2015).

I hope you enjoy this book as much as I love bringing it to you.

Dr. Alkhatani Saad Zafer

1

Introduction

1.1 Defining Customer Centricity

With the advances of technologies, businesses are being influenced to migrate from a product centric into a customer centric approach. Business orientation has been evolving from a purely production growth focus in 1900's, to a sales growth focus until the 1950's, to a marketing driven focus by 2000, and to a customer centric focus in the recent past (Ranjit, 2002). This shift has occurred due to the strengthening of economies and the tightening of competition due to an increased number of suppliers of competitive goods and services in the market.

In a world where customer expectations are constantly changing and competition is always growing, companies are under increasing pressure to become customer-centric. Bailey (2006) suggests that the first step to become a customer-centric organization is to define what it means to your organization. He defines customer centricity as "Aligning the resources of your organization to effectively respond to the ever changing needs of the customer while building a mutually profitable relationship."

More than 50 years ago Drucker (1954) wrote in his book, *The Practice of Management*, that "it is the customer who determines what a business is,

Authentic Customer Centricity, pages 1–12
Copyright © 2015 by Information Age Publishing
All rights of reproduction in any form reserved.

what it produces and whether it will prosper." The Booz Allen Hamilton report (2004) distinguishes the customer-centric organization from other companies that proclaim their customer centricity by moving beyond lip service and re-oriented their entire operating model around the customer. This report defines the concept of customer centric companies as those who "understand not only the meaning of customer values, but also the value the customer represents to their bottom line."

The report added that customer-centric organizations are characterized by clear and aligned operation models which are linked to a carefully defined and quantified customer segmentation strategy. This segmentation strategy is designed to deliver the greatest value to the best customers for the least cost.

The American Productivity Quality Center (APQC) report (2001) stated that "There is no one agreed upon definition for customer-centricity, although consistent characteristics are found among best practice organizations." However, the same report characterized customer-centric companies as those who are built around the ideal experience of the customer.

Jay (2005) defines customer centric companies as those organizations which consist of structure, business processes, management practice, reward systems and human resources procedures, that are aligned around the customer's needs and expectations. In the same vein, Ron (2006) stated that "customer-centric business puts customer needs and desires at the center of their entire operations, from technical support to marketing, and even new product and service decisions."

The latter definitions of both Jay (2005) and Ron (2006) are in line with Bailey's definition of customer centricity as "Aligning the resources of your organization to effectively respond to the ever changing needs of the customers while building mutually profitable relationship." It seems that there is a common understanding among different authors in defining customer centricity, most of them have concluded that in being customer centric, all business activities, offerings, services and products have to be based on the customer's needs rather than the requirements of internal processes and systems.

Three major cores of the successful management from this point of view are the positive customer experience satisfaction which help customer retention and win business for the company. As Reichheld and Sasser have proven already in 1990, retaining customers and increasing their loyalty are much less costly for the company than acquiring new customers (Reichheld and Sasser, 1990). The second core is the employee satisfaction within this organization, leading to the third core, namely, devotion of the staff at all hierarchy levels to turning organization operations into customer centric organization. This chapter sheds light on these customer centricity constituents.

1.2 Evolution of Customer Centricity

Customer centricity, as a concept that we know of today, was introduced in 1990s with the technological advancements in database industry. But it is actually not a new idea. It has been around for many years in different forms. At its most basic level the seller matching the offer the buyer's demand. This concept has been around since mankind discovered the advantages of trading (Bailey, 2006). It is dated back to Mesopotamians when they started to farm their land. These early famers realized that they were producing more than they could eat and so they started to trade. Early merchants kept accurate business records to keep track of what products were sold to which customers, by what quantities and when, so that they could produce more of selling items during the times customers needed them.

The small grocery store on the corner of the street used to know the names of its customers, their preferred brands and their buying habits. It used to stock the favorite brand of cookies to selective customers so that they could buy them every time they wanted to and even delivered them to their homes on their preferred time. Together with industrial revolution, small grocery stores like those left their places to big super market chains who did not know who the customers were and didn't care what their individual preferences were as long as they were selling enough products to make big profits. Mass marketers were attempting to sell products through persuasion by broadcasting a message hoping to reach as much customers as they could to sell their "one size fits all" products.

Henry Ford's, father of mass production, famous quote "Any customer can have a car in any color that he wants as long as it is black" for Ford Model T summarizes the marketing strategy of 1920s product driven companies. As it became important for suppliers to learn what their customers demand to stay alive in the competition, marketers started studying market segmentation to learn more about their customers and their needs as smaller groups based on variables such as demographic, geographic and psychographic variables. In 1960, initiating a new approach to customer centricity, Theodore (1960) famously stated "People don't want to buy a quarter-inch drill, they want a quarter-inch hole." and opened the eyes of marketers who were focusing too much on creating products for narrow demographic segments rather than satisfying individual customer needs.

Together with the advancements in technology, the importance of knowledge on customers came into focus. It enabled companies to do business in the oldest fashioned ways by making it possible to remember individual relationships with millions of customers. The eighties where the years when database marketing started enabling companies, no matter what their sizes were, to store their customers' information. However, it was too costly for most companies by that time to collect data on customer purchases and the return on investment was not as high. Even the companies that could afford the new technology were mostly using customer information only as a one way road to better market their products. American Airlines was one of the first to realize the real potential of knowing customers and their values, by not only knowing what they demand but also turning them into loyal customers that always choose their services even when the prices are a little higher. They decided to take advantage of this and launched their frequent flyer program to help retaining their best customers by giving them back in terms of free upgrades and tickets.

At the beginning of nineties Don and Martha (1993) introduced the concept of "one-to-one marketing" and Michael and James (1993) wrote about customer centric business models. They introduced customer centricity as an organizational structure rather than just a marketing tool. During these years an unparalleled technological revolution took place. With communications technologies, such as internet, becoming more and more available, free information exchange rate increased enormously leading to a commoditization process. This caused a reduction in the profit margins in many marketplaces. Suppliers' need for finding alternative ways of keeping profits high, combined with now more affordable database marketing tools, opened the doors for true customer centricity. Suppliers, who previously were only trying to know more about customers' buying habits to better market their products, now want to create a two way communication to learn more about customer needs and their preferences. "Database Marketing" turned into "Database Relationship". Loyalty programs became more and more popular and customer centricity grew into specialist areas such as contact management, customer service and customer value analysis (Bailey, 2006).

During early nineties, computer systems were used to support sales and service processes. More and more companies started to use these systems to create automated sales forces systems and customer service and support systems became the backbone of automated call centers. In mid-nineties, customer relationship management systems were started to be used as a linkage between sales and service departments, sharing the customer information to provide a single view of customer and enhance the relation with them. During this time, many companies found out that they knew much less about their own customers than they thought they did. In an attempt to increase customer satisfaction and loyalty in 1996, Royal Bank of Canada (RBC) opened more branches, extended working hours and installed many ATMs to create a convenient banking experience for its customers. But it was to their surprise that their customers were not choosing a bank for its convenience but rather based on how much their business was valued (Michael and James, 1993).

With increased usage of internet during late nineties, CRM systems were enhanced to handle e-business applications making it possible to give same high quality service to customers, preserving the same single company face, no matter which communication mode they chose to use. With the advancement in wireless technologies, such as cellular phones, organizations have more possibilities than ever to connect with their customers and build strong relationships increasing value of each customer.

Today, it is clearer that it is the organizations, and not the marketing departments that shape and drive the brand. Getting close to customers in not so much a problem the IT or marketing department needs to solve as a journey that the whole organization needs to make (Ranjay and James, 2005). Becoming a truly customer centric organization requires changing the whole culture of how they do business. Now, understanding the customers through CRM systems are being followed by designing value chains around customer experiences and aligning the organization around it and still being able to be profitable.

1.3 Product Centricity versus Customer Centricity

Technically, customer centricity is a hybrid form of revolution and evolution of a product centricity paradigm. Product by definition captures customer centric elements otherwise there would be no transaction or trade between customers and businesses, i.e., no willingness to purchase to fulfill a demand. Historically, firms have tended to be product centric (Denish et al., 2006), because profits were primarily a reflection of market share (Buzzell and Gale, 1987). As a result, firms were more internally oriented, with their attention focused on manufacturing high quality products rather than being oriented toward the purchaser and users of those products or services (Levitt, 1960). In short, production efficiency possesses the highest priority. A product centric company draws its foundation from the early years of marketing. The first marketing scholars directed their emphasis toward commodities exchange. Denish et al. (2006) and Jay (2005) revealed that a product centric company tries to look for as many users and customers as possible for its products and services. In contrast, a customer centric company tries to find as many products or services as possible for its customers (Jay, 2005). He characterized the product centric firms by being structured around the product profit centers, called business units, while the customer centric firms are structured around the customer segments.

A customer centric company focuses on the processes and technology that support and enhance a customer centric strategy. A customer centric organization establishes an operational value chain against customer touch points, captures the needs of customers, and readies the company for the potential wishes of customers given the market trends and forces. These companies realize that process and technology changes are the corner stone of becoming a truly customer centric organization (APQC, 2001). Denish et al. (2006) added that the true essence of the customer centricity paradigm lies not in how to sell services or products but rather on creating value from both the customer and the company; in other words customer centricity is related to the process of dual value creation. A customer centric organization prices its offering on the basis of the value it creates to customers and not on the basis of market condition (Jay, 2005).

A good comparison of a product centric and a customer centric organization is summarized in Table 1.1. It gives a good idea of what a customer centric organization looks like and how close or how far a company is from that model.

1.4 The Importance of Customer Centricity

Customers are the life and blood of any company and the heart of the demand-driven economy. They are critical for the survival of a firm and the most valuable asset; as a result, companies have to move quickly toward the customer centricity approach (Gupta et al., 2004). To become a customer centric organization, a company needs to be capable of providing the right customer experience at the right time. The rise of the customer centricity dimension is motivated by the increasing buyer-power influence—and the correct thinking that this is where longevity, competitive edge and financial profitability lie (Jay, 2005). He added that there are specific factors causing the increased importance of customer centricity to organization, namely, the globalization of customer, the preference of customers for partnership or relationships, the rise of e-commerce, the customers' desire for customized solutions. Fierce competition in most of the markets has derived the implementation of customer centricity very quickly. Hewlett-Packard, for example, has reorganized its structure several timed to meet the needs of its customers, it named top level managers of total customer experience for both its

TABLE 1.1   A Comparison of the Product-Centric and Customer-Centric Approaches

	Product-Centric Approach	Customer-Centric Approach
Basic philosophy	Sell products; we'll sell to whoever will buy	Service consumers; all decisions start with the customer and opportunities for advantage
Business orientation	Transaction oriented	Relationship oriented
Product positioning	Highlight product features and advantages	Highlight product's benefits in terms of meeting individual customer needs
Organizational structure	Product profit centers, product managers, products sales team	Customer segment centers, customer relationship managers, customer segment sales team
Organizational focus	Internally focused, new products developed, new account developed, market share growth; customer relations are issues for the marketing department	Externally focused, customer relationship department, profitability through customer loyalty; employees are customer advocates
Performance metrics	Number of new products, profitability per product, market share by product/subbrands	Share of wallet of customers, customer satisfaction, customer lifetime value, customer equity
Management criteria	Portfolio of products	Portfolio of customers
Selling approach	How many customers can we sell this product to?	How many products can we sell this customer?
Customer knowledge	Customer data are a control mechanism	Customer knowledge is valuable asset

Source: (Shah et al., 2006)

consumers and field operations. It implemented a blended channel strategy that gives the consumers the flexibility to switch back and forth from the web to the phone, as well as to other media and it restructured the managers' bonuses to reflect their units' customer experience scores (David, 2007).

Total customer experience is a key source of competitive differentiation in the constantly evolving markets. By excelling at the strategic customer centric imperatives, companies can deliver a superior customer experience that could not only result in constantly high customer relations but also increase in customer loyalty and profitability (IBM, 2005).

Companies can no longer rely on the traditional means of competitive differentiation. For example, strategies based just on price are ineffective.

More information about the customer needs and expectations are more vital for the success of many products and services. Today's information and technology survey customers demand more from the shopping experience. They are often more knowledgeable than companies' employees about available products, services and prices. Companies and their sales employees need to know more about their customers to deliver a superior customer experience to them (Gina et al., 2005). Critical strategic imperatives for customer centricity were defined by Gina et al. (2005) as four main factors. The first one is the importance to build the organization offering based on a customer experience that evolves with changing customer expectations and needs. The entire organization must focus on identifying, satisfying and responding to the target customers' rapidly evolving needs and preferences. The second imperative is the need to provide a truly convenient shopping experience; this shopping experience keeps customers coming back. Customers want a company that is easy to deal with and requires less time and effort. The third imperative is the need for organization to have a holistic view of the customers. Eliminating customer data silos that can lead to inconsistent versions of customer data and letting the customers to decide how much intimacy they want or need is an essential imperative for company to reach to the customer centricity level they want to be. The fourth imperative is organizations are struggling to deliver flexible products or services that meet their target customers.

Companies must address customer needs and preferences across several areas, including target segments, local markets, shopping occasions and service categories. To deliver flexible offerings companies are required to address four key steps namely, understanding target customers and their wants and preferences, develop deeper insight about their customers interactions, leverage these insights to tailor products and services to the needs of target customers. Finally, build a team of skilled sales employees that can provide the level of service which meets different customers' needs.

The case study presented by Booz Allen (2003) about the customer centric bank, revealed that banks need to understand how to build interactive relationships and that is a social sciences concept called the "Johari Window". It describes interpersonal communication in term of four major quadrants: open, blind, unknown and hidden (see Figure 1.1). To develop true relationships with customers, banks need to maximize the open quadrant of shared information. Today, the only information shared with customers are bank statements, loan applications, credit contracts and service requests as shown in Figure 1.1.

Banks need to enlarge this open window to include information in the Hidden Quadrant i.e., known only to the customer such as life stage, wealth

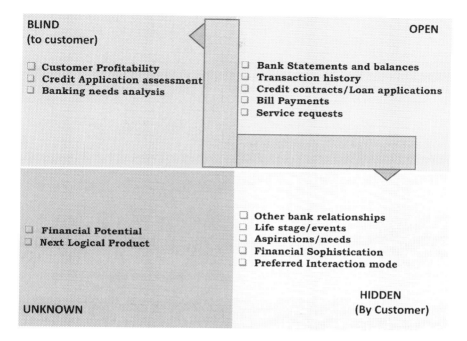

Figure 1.1 Retail Banking Johan Window (Booz Allen, 2003).

goals and preferred mode of interaction. In the same time banks should leverage the information in the Blind Quadrant i.e., known only to the bank, to educate customers and win their trust. The Johan window has created a need for organizations to open a dialogue with their customers and build with them a genuine interactive relationship through adopting a truly customer centric strategy (Booz Allen, 2003). The customer imperatives that Gina et al. (2005) identified and the findings of the case study of Booz Allen (2003) for specific bank are more related to the surrounding conditions of the research as well as the companies' environment under study. It would be useful to identify the management and front line employees point of view of the importance of customer centricity to their company and relate them to the competition environment of the market.

The measurable results of a customer-centric mindset often emanate from financial investment in business process improvements that are directly made as a result of the customers' unmet needs, preferences and requirements. These types of investments often occur at a very fundamental, systemic level in organizations in order to make their entire series of databases, systems and programs all align to the needs of customers (Reychav and Weisberg, 2009). The need to make customer-centricity a foundational element in any process improvements is directly tied to customer loyalty and achieved long-term cost reductions (Reichheld, Markey Jr., and Hopton, 2000). Investing in driving up loyalty by getting key customer criteria from a process standpoint can not only make an organization easier to do business with, but can also increase loyalty as well (Reichheld and Detrick, 2003).

As Harvard Business Review elaborates: "By describing the landscape of unmet customer needs and analyzing where new offerings have worked before, you can chart a path that will produce successful innovations time after time" (Anthony, Eyring, and Gibson 2006, p. 31). An APQC (2001) report reveals that a customer-centric company focuses on the processes and technology that support and enhance a customer-centric strategy. They realize that process and technology changes are the cornerstone of becoming a truly customer-centric organization.

Shook (2009) believes that customer-centricity plays a very critical role in organizational effectiveness, one that impacts the return on investment and hence shareholder value. Figure 1.2 shows the relationships of these factors and highlights why it is so critical for customer-centricity to drive organizational effectiveness investment strategies.

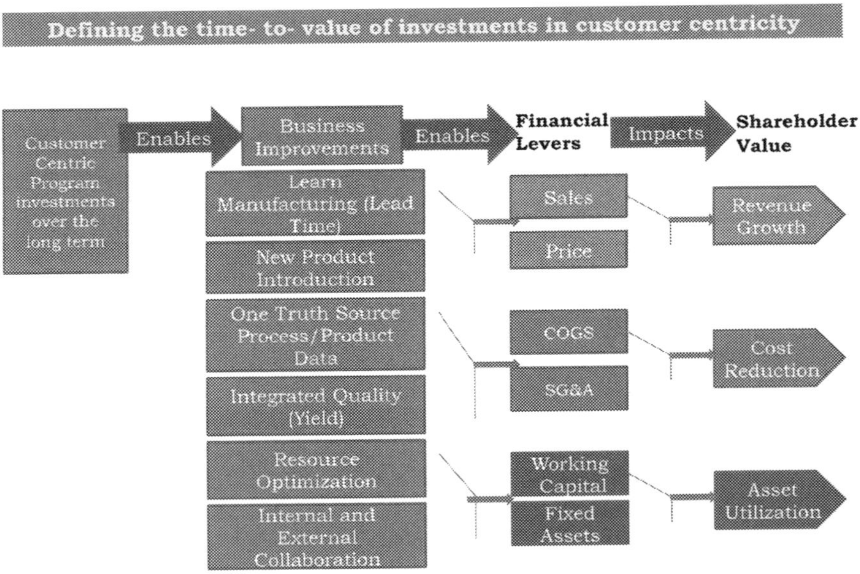

Figure 1.2 Evaluating the value chain of time-to-value investments in customer-centricity (Shah et al., 2006)

Dyer and Nobeoka (2000) and Shah et al. (2006) agree that improving organizational effectiveness begins by taking the perspectives and insights from customers and acting on them. As Prahalad and Ramaswamy (2000) note, today customers buy more than just a product; personalization and customization are necessary. Eric and Linda (2006) explain that a customer-centric organization sees customers as individuals, men and women who make their own lifestyle choices and who come from a variety of backgrounds. They added that marketing managers must look at the varied cultures and subcultures that make up the whole that is the marketplace. In the same context, Peltier et al. (2006) add that individual consumers will demand certain goods and services. Their inquiries will further stimulate the creation of new business models and permit companies to grow and eventually expand in new and possibly undreamed of directions. Shook (2009) states that customer-centric organizations, therefore, mark excellence in understanding and reacting to changing market needs from a customer's perspective. Dyer and Nobeoka (2000) and Shah et al. (2006) conclude that customer-centric organizations have fully integrated processes that tie in customer understanding with all business functions. Processes in these organizations are also perfectly consistent and drive customer satisfaction and loyalty.

A Booz Allen Hamilton (2003) report stresses that companies must address customer needs and preferences across several areas, including target segments, local markets, shopping occasions and service categories. To deliver flexible offerings, companies are required to address four key steps: understanding target customers and their wants, needs and preferences; developing deeper insight into their customers' interactions; leveraging these insights to tailor products and services to the needs of target customers; and building a team of skilled sales employees and robust support systems and processes that can provide the level of service that meets different customers' needs. Reichheld and Detrick (2003) stress that the impact of customer-centricity on organizations ultimately makes them more profitable not only from the loyalty effect aspect, but also through their more effective and efficient processes in addressing customer needs.

Capturing and addressing customer requirements are a critical quest for businesses to create sustainable customer centric value chain and operations. This book gives you the necessary building blocks for a successful and effective journey in migrating product centric organization into a customer centric one. Chapter 2 emphasizes the introduction of an authentic customer centricity model, which provides a roadmap to develop, implement, and cultivate customer centricity in a sustainable way. Employee satisfaction has a major impact on building customer centric organization and customer centricity. Because happy employees lead directly to happy customers. Chapter 3 describes personal centricity which focuses on employee satisfaction. Chapter 4 focuses on corporate centricity; the processes and technology that support and enhance a customer centric strategy. Good strategic alignment has a strong effect on organizational performance and is essential for becoming a sustainable customer centric company. People perform better when they fully understand and accept the purpose and goals of their organization, and they develop a better sense of ownership when they understand what difference they make in achieving those goals. It enables higher performance by optimizing the contributions of people, processes, and inputs to the realization of measurable objectives. Chapter 5 describes this strategic alignment process. Chapter 6 emphasizes the cultivation of customer experience and in Chapter 7 I will discuss a business case to illustrate the concept of customer centricity.

2

Authentic Customer Centricity Model

In this chapter I launch an authentic customer centricity model, which provides a practical and effective framework for blending the aspects of individuals and corporate elements with the strategy and cultivating this effectively. It's derived from Hubert Rampersad's Authentic Branding model (Rampersad, 2008, 2015).

The authentic customer centricity model consists of four phases (see Figure 2.1), which are the building blocks of a sustainable customer centricity organization:

1. *Personal centricity*; employee satisfaction has a major impact on building customer centric organization and customer centricity. Because respect for employees leads directly to respect for customers. Dissatisfied personnel will not care to correct mistakes or to deal properly with outside customers. The customer centric approach therefore dictates a concern for every aspect of the business process, from the lowest-level employee on up the line to the

Authentic Customer Centricity, pages 13–15
Copyright © 2015 by Information Age Publishing
All rights of reproduction in any form reserved.

Figure 2.1 Authentic Customer Centricity Model.

most high-powered levels. This phase emphasis on the elements that are related to employee satisfaction.

2. *Corporate centricity;* this phase involves integrating customer centricity strategy, organizational processes, structure and information technology so that the whole organization will move towards customer centricity.

3. *Strategic alignment;* alignment is the adjustment of an object in relation to other objects so that the arrangement can lead to the optimizing of the position or the relationship between the objects. Strategic alignment is the process of aligning an organization's structure and resources with its strategy and business environment. It is a business redesign process, in which you align your strategic goals (= what do we want to achieve?), business processes (= how do we want to achieve it?), and company culture with your key business purpose (= why are we here?) and core values (= which are the values and behaviors in line with our purpose?). It is also about bringing the actions of an organization's business divisions and staff members in line with the organization's planned objectives, in order to assure that its divisions and employees are jointly working toward the company's stated goals. Good strategic alignment has a strong effect on organizational performance and is essential for becoming a sustainable customer centric company. People perform better when they fully understand and accept

the purpose and goals of their organization, and they develop a better sense of ownership when they understand what difference they make in achieving those goals (Rampersad, 2003). It enables higher performance by optimizing the contributions of people, processes, and inputs to the realization of measurable objectives. With strategic alignment, it is possible to improve customer satisfaction more effectively and gain a competitive advantage.

4. *Cultivation*; the effective combination of all these four phases creates a stable basis for a high-performance customer experience. This experience occurs at every and each touch point such as contact centers, sales people, advertising, events and others. The customer experience is filtered through customers' expectation of the company which is determined by the customer's value proposition and feedback from other customers.

As we can see from Figure 2.1, the model gives us insight into both the way authentic customer centricity can be developed effectively and the coherence between its different aspects. After the last phase is completed, the cycle is again followed in order to fine tune the elements with its surroundings on a continuous basis. By doing this you will constantly improve the customer centricity of your organization on an ongoing basis. Your organization will also constantly improve its performance and continuously add value to its clients.

3

Personal Centricity

This chapter emphasizes personal centricity, which is the first stage in the authentic customer centricity journey (see Figure 3.1). Employee satisfaction has a major impact on building customer centric organization and customer centricity, because respect for employees leads directly to respect for customers (Rampersad, 2015). Dissatisfied personnel will not care to correct mistakes or to deal properly with customers. The customer centric approach therefore dictates a concern for every aspect of the business on all levels and is strongly related to employee satisfaction.

3.1 Customer Satisfaction and Employee Satisfaction

Customer satisfaction and employee satisfaction are two dual measures for an organization's success. The customer looks at the organization from the outside, while the employee views it from within and both intrinsically gauge how organization is progressing. As described by Andy (2002), the well-functioning organization owes its success to the inputs of an extensive range of disciplines: accounting, operations management, marketing, finance, economics, psychology and sociology. Each of these fields contrib-

Authentic Customer Centricity, pages 17–42
Copyright © 2015 by Information Age Publishing
All rights of reproduction in any form reserved.

Figure 3.1 First stage in the Authentic Customer Centricity model (derived from Rampersad, 2015).

utes in some measure to customer satisfaction and employee satisfaction. Accounting, marketing, finance and economics in general, represent mathematical calculations of a company's or customer's bottom line. These disciplines address the practical side of getting to the customer the things that he or she needs or wants. On the other hand, psychology and sociology, and in some respects, operation management and marketing, examine business and customer behaviours as a matter of interaction between individuals and groups. Emotions frequently come into play, as do the positive and negative feedbacks that accrue from a job well-rewarded or a service ineptly provided. Marketing and operations management represent the intersection of these objective and subjective approaches. In marketing a good or service, one often appeals to the feelings in order to sell a tangible product. In running a factory or office, an operations manager deals with personnel as operators of machinery or furnishers of services, in other words, as human resources that perform specified functions. That same operations manager, however, must also consider those employees as living breathing men and women; men and women with families, feelings and personal preferences that may have little or nothing to do with the specifications of a piece of equipment or the needs of an assembly line of corporate board room.

These quantitative and qualitative attributes come together in the mind of the customer as in the mind of the employee. The work by Anders and Michael (2000) depict customer satisfaction as a complex set of perceptions:

The way the customer perceives the concrete attributes of a product, the benefits the customer derives from those attributes, and the personal values that the product supports. All these elements reside with the customer and are beyond the company's direct control...

Though not under the company's direct control, these attributes are nevertheless capable of being influenced by the proper procedures and considerations. The customer-centric organization recognizes that a company and its employees can make decisions and implement practices that can indirectly mould the perceptions of end customers. Under these conditions, knowledge of customer behaviour is especially important. Psychology and its allied disciplines offer a window on the cognitive processes that lead to the development of specific attitudes and preferences on the part of consumers. Consumer surveys and other analytical studies can help marketers to understand what affects consumer choices, and how customers fit into different categories according to age, sex, social and income status, and so forth. Much of marketing can be related to the ideas of social identity theory. Social identity theory states that individuals are continually endeavouring to shape their identity, or identities, for according to this theory, an individual possesses multiple self-images that fit different situations. By placing the customer at the center of the operational paradigm, customer centrism declares the necessity of comprehending these different customer selves.

As well, social identity theory is applicable to the employees of a company. Employees, like the customers they serve, constitute a discreet social group or set. Sharing a common environment, they interact in what students of social behaviour term an "arena." Arenas are social groupings that create and enforce socially constructed rules and procedures that represent the social identity of participants and the appropriateness of their activities (Theresa and Zur, 2001). In other words, a company is a form of social organization that governs the conduct of its members and in which the employees act in line with the formulated rules. These rules may include not merely the specific regulations enacted by management, but also the collective responsive of employees to external stimuli, as for example, communications from customers. However, ad-hoc decisions can become a kind of precedent that establishes environmental norms within the organization. An example might be a case where particular customers' complaints are handled in a certain manner not regulated by any official company regulations. An auto manufacturer employee responds to complaints about late deliveries by claiming that an essential part has been held up at customs. This excuse becomes standard operating procedure in this and all similar situations. Such an example also provides insight into the development of potential problems in dealing with customers.

Central to consumers' decisions to purchase a product or service is the process of goal setting. With goal setting, the consumer identifies specific aims that are to be achieved through the use of the given good or service (Richard, and Utpal, 2004). A television is purchased in order to enable the customer to watch various programs. The consumer may look for any number generally popular or personally important features. Surround sound, multiple pictures in picture capability and HDTV may all be considered features of importance when determining which TV set to obtain. In that case, the real goal of the customer is not so much the purchase of a device that permits her or him to watch her or his favourite shows, but rather the procuring of a television with all of the newest and most fashionable technological features. Understanding the real goal that the customer has set is an important part of learning to work with goal setting theory. It is also an example of how the customer centric business strives to look at the entire process from the customer's point of view. Knowing the customer's point of view entails being able to examine that viewpoint from every conceivable angle, and being able to predict for such.

Therefore, the ability to understand all of the implications of goal setting for the customer requires a similar ability in regard to the organization's own personnel. A first goal of any customer centric business is serving the customer. Everything a company does must be geared to achieving this goal. The enterprise needs to be organized in such a way that the customer's interests are never sacrificed to those of the employees. The customer is always right. Nevertheless, such an attitude demands its own subsidiary goals. If the aims of the organization include the achievement of a high level customer service, employees' tasks and routines must similarly be conductive to satisfying the customer. The work by Jim, Olga and Mary, (2005) identify the characteristics of decision-making that tend to enhance an organization's ability to be customer centric. As with all decisions, the decision-maker must be able to make judgments that satisfy objective as well as subjective requirements.

A decision maker operating in a complex, dynamic task environment should be thought of as an engineer endeavouring to control a complex dynamic system, a key element of which is the decision maker's own self-regulatory processes. Thus, self-monitoring and self-regulation processes are a source of feedback about the effectiveness of the decision maker's adaptive task system. (Jim, Olga and Mary, 2005).

The goals that must be met on the employee side of the equation are real-world aims. The solutions that accomplish them must be real-world solutions. Essentially, Jim, Olga and Mary (2005) distinguish between the decision-maker who operates largely, or exclusively, in the realm of theory as opposed to the realist who closely examines the actual effects of a policy. Implicit here is the belief that policies must be tested before they are implemented or, at the very least, altered after implementation if they are found wanting or ineffective. The customer centric approach encourages the testing of new or amended policies in real-world solutions.

In its widest possible sense, the belief of customer centrism embraces every aspect of the modern business paradigm. Employees expect decent working conditions and a business environment that makes sense. If personnel do not understand instructions, or do not comprehend the goals of given policies and procedures they will not be productive and will be unable to adequately serve the company's customer base. Furthermore, employees who are not properly compensated and rewarded are not obtaining their desired level of "customer" satisfaction within the work environment. Consumer centric organizations must set as their company-wide goal the aim of high human performance and they must insure that their employees gain a sense of satisfaction in return for their efforts. Employee satisfaction will derive from giving employees personally meaningful work that they are capable of handling and from rewarding good performance (Rampersad, 2015). The best American organizations have organizational philosophies that place a high premium on excellence in performance and on respect for employees. (John, 2002). Respect for employees leads directly to respect for customers. As in the theoretic example given above, the offering of excuses to customers does not bode well for the creation of good customer relationships. In similar vein, a company that mistreats its employees, or keeps them ill-informed, or cut out of the decision-making process, is a company that is almost certain to damage its relationships with its clients. Dissatisfied personnel will not care to correct mistakes or to deal properly with outside customers. They will not put in extra amount of time and effort for the company. The organization's bottom line will be adversely affected. The customer centric approach dictates a concern for every aspect of the business process, from the lowest-level employee on up the line to the most high-powered levels. In the following section the relationship between customer centricity and employee satisfaction will be discussed in detail.

3.2 Employee Satisfaction and Customer Centricity

As employee satisfaction is tightly correlated with customer satisfaction, it is an instrumental building for organizations to be able to achieve a customer centricity setup. In this paragraph I will provide necessary frameworks and instruments that link employee satisfaction with customer centricity.

3.2.1 The Hackman and Oldham Model Theories of Employee Satisfaction

Processes within organizations must be designed to meet not only the technical demands but also the human capital needs. If processes are also designed to fulfill the needs of employees, motivation will increase, leading to an improvement in quality and work force productivity. The underlying principle behind the Hackman and Oldham Model (see Figure 3.2), incorporates both the technical and mental elements of job design. Evans and Lindsay (1996) confirm that the Hackman and Oldham model is a further development and operationalization of Herzberg's theory, and has been validated in many different organizational settings. Evans and Lindsay also mention that employee satisfaction can be improved if the job design incorporates empowerment and involvement, process ownership, job enlargement/rotation and feedback about performance.

Employees can derive satisfaction from their jobs by meeting or exceeding the emotional wants and needs they expect from their work (Pepitone, 2006). Therefore, managers that recognize this and understand the different aspects that are involved in employee satisfaction will be successful at

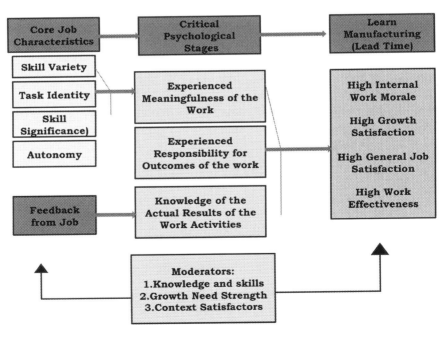

Figure 3.2 Hackman and Oldham's Work Design model (Evans & Lindsay, 1996).

achieving the link between employee satisfaction, customer retention and profitability. As previously stated, the issue of employee satisfaction has a major impact on building a customer centric organization. In the next section I will comprehensively analyze the important elements that are related to employee satisfaction.

3.2.2 Work Environment

Studies show that employees who feel "empowered" are productive employees. According to Ronald J. Burke and Cary L. Cooper (2004), the idea that employee empowerment can lead to positive outcomes is not unique to the service context, as evidenced by the widespread acceptance of the job characteristics model according to which enriched jobs (characterized by greater autonomy, variety, task identity and significance, and performance feedback) are associated with positive work outcomes and employee satisfaction.

Employees are often placed under considerable pressures in today's fast-paced and constantly changing business environment. Corporate buy-outs and take-overs bring sudden changes in management personnel and style, in company goals and business techniques—all things which employees are required to adjust themselves to without further consideration, thus creating a rapidly changing emotional cycle that unfortunately is not as flexible as the business cycle to which it is attached (Marc, 2004). These sudden pressures of another emotional cycle notwithstanding, the ordinary pressures of the workplace compounded with lack of communication, unintelligible procedures, too heavy workloads, etc. can also lead directly to loss of productivity and to problems with customers. This can lead to burnout, which is a psychological process that results in emotional exhaustion, depersonalization, and feelings of decreased accomplishment. The result of this is long periods of unrelieved job stress and decreased employee performance, higher absenteeism, and high levels of turnover (John and Lucy, 1998).

A customer-centric organization must be as concerned with the atmosphere it furnishes its employees as with the shopping or service environment it provides to its clientele. The two are interdependent. In particular, the consumer will suffer if the employee's basic needs are not being met. The single most important factor contributing to employee satisfaction is the internal quality of the work environment. The respect and appreciation employees derive from their co-workers and employers helps to determine the internal work environment (Stein and Book, 2000). The term "work environment" encompasses many different aspects such as: physical work environment, management's attitude toward employees, relationship with colleagues, and working conditions. Recent research has highlighted the hypothesis that an employee's work environment can have a dramatic effect on his/her performance and attitude toward work. For example, one's workspace has traditionally been conceptualized as just a passive host to its user activities. However, it is now recognized that the space workers occupy at work effects patterns of interaction, and can have a noticeable impact on behavior and performance.

Management must strive to always be aware of toxic relationships, tense behavior between employees, and negative overtones in the work environment. By creating positive environments that nurture success, employers are exhibiting to their employees a commitment to achieving an atmosphere that will engender employee satisfaction in the workplace.

3.2.3 *Recognition*

Employees were once thought to be just a normal part of the production process of creating goods and services. Today however, most organizations realize that employees are much more than just "input" as part of the business generation process, and require motivation and subsequent recognition in order to build and maintain employee satisfaction. In this section I will consider the different methods associated with motivating and recognizing employees, in order to achieve maximum employee satisfaction. Much of the basis for employee motivation can be traced to the Hawthorne studies, conducted by Elton Mayo from 1924 to 1932. The major conclusion of this study was that employees are not solely motivated by money and employer behavior and attitude have a great deal to do with an employee's satisfaction. After this initial research, understanding employee motivation was the focus of many other researchers, the most notably being Maslow, who developed the need-hierarchy theory. According to A.H. Maslow, people's needs resemble a pyramid. As basic needs are satisfied, higher levels of needs emerge and motivate the employee's behavior. Because of this, organizations need to provide a work environment that will motivate employees above and beyond their physiological and safety needs (John, 2006). The analysis in regard to this topic will be done using the analysis and research presented in Maslow's hierarchy of needs theory (see Figure 3.3).

Motivation has been defined somewhat differently by many different researchers, but is generally accepted as: the psychological process that gives behavior purpose and direction; a predisposition to behave in a purposive manner to achieve specific, unmet needs; an internal drive to satisfy an unsatisfied need; and the will to achieve (Lindner, 1998). Motivation is here operationally defined as the inner force that drives individuals to accomplish personal and organizational goals. Having established a working definition for "motivation", the next step is to assess the role of motivation

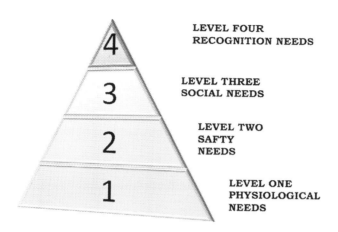

MASALOW'S HIERARCHY OF NEEDS

LEVEL FOUR
RECOGNITION NEEDS

LEVEL THREE
SOCIAL NEEDS

LEVEL TWO
SAFTY
NEEDS

LEVEL ONE
PHYSIOLOGICAL
NEEDS

Figure 3.3 Maslow's Hierarchy of Needs (John Gray Awards).

in moving organizations to be more customer focus. The obvious question that must be asked before assessing the role of motivations in organizations is, "why is it necessary or important to motivate employees?" The answer is one of economics. Motivated employees are more productive, more engaged, and are satisfied workers. Employees that are motivated have a sense of purpose and belonging, and therefore tend to exhibit greater loyalty to their respective organizations.

A good example of an organization proactively assessing the factors that motivate their employees can be found at the Piketon Research and Extension Center in Piketon, Ohio. The Company developed a survey questionnaire consisting of ten factors and asked employees to rank them in order of importance. A comparison of these results to Maslow's need-hierarchy theory provides some interesting insight into employee motivation. The number one ranked motivator, interesting work, is a self-actualizing factor. The number two-ranked motivator, good wages, is a physiological factor. The number three-ranked motivator, full appreciation of work done, is an esteem factor. The number four-ranked motivator, job security, is a safety factor. Therefore, according to Maslow (1943), if managers wish to address the most important motivational factor of the Center employees, interesting work, physiological safety, social, and esteem factors must first be satisfied. As is the case in this example, an employee survey can help management effectively identify the factors that they should consider in order to better motivate their employees.

An integral part of employee motivation is making it constant and perpetual and one of the best ways to accomplish this is with a formal employee recognition program. Recognizing and applauding employees' achievements and contributions are critical to reinforcing desired behaviors. The best way to encourage desired behavior and create enthusiasm for continued future improvement is to formally recognize employees. Recognition programs have proven to play an important role in a company's employee satisfaction and creating a customer centric environment. Recognition programs serve to create positive environments that encourage desired behaviors. Organizations that implement meaningful and effective recognition programs often gain a competitive edge through increased employee retention and an increase in overall employee satisfaction (Reche, 2006).

The implementation of effective award and recognition programs can create a positive working environment that encourages employees to thrive. Recognition makes employees feel valued and appreciated, it contributes to higher employee morale, and increases organizational productivity. In addition, strong recognition programs are effective employee motivation tools. They work to reinforce organizational goals, mission, and vision (Brintnall, 2005). In a recent Gallup poll survey of 80,000 employees, recognition ranked fourth among the 12 dimensions that consistently correlated with those workgroups that have higher employee retention (Gallup, 2006). The key to recognition programs being successful is to formalize them and make them a priority, like any other corporate goal.

The important point to keep in mind regarding recognition programs is that they come in all shapes and sizes and do not have to be expensive to initiate. The most important factors are that they must be fair, consistent, and valued by the employees. Effective recognition does not necessarily have to be in the form of monetary remuneration, but must be tangible and appreciated by employees. Most employee surveys indicate that their organization lacks an effective recognition program, and also that recognition programs are valuable at increasing employee satisfaction. Organizations that are able to implement effective recognition programs often benefit from higher employee morale, increased productivity, and a general increase in overall employee satisfaction as well as customer satisfaction (Reche, 2006).

3.2.4 Communication

The art of communication is a vital component of employee satisfaction and engagement. Without workplace communication, nothing would be accomplished. Instructions could not be given, equipment and supplies could not be ordered, progress could not be measured, and services could not be delivered to customers. The five functions of management: planning, organizing, staffing, leading, and controlling, are all dependent on communication. Surveys conducted with highly successful managers consistently highlight the benefits of effective communication (Slagle, 2006). There are many different methods of communicating in the workplace that include: face-to-face meetings, staff meetings, small group meetings, department meetings, management forum meetings, walkabouts, telephone conversations, mission statements, newsletters, bulletin boards, e-mail, and intranets, just to name a few. All other components of this analysis would be impossible to implement without communication. For that reason, this section will be concerned with employee communication in the workplace, and the many considerations involved with effectively communicating at work that contributes greatly in building customer centric organization.

Employees communicate with each other and management in many different ways, as well as being communicated to by management in many different ways. Employee communication is a very powerful factor in the level of employee satisfaction that workers in an organization have. From the perspective of the employee, communication from management is a re-affirmation of what the leadership believes and stands for. For this reason, the effectiveness and efficiency of communication in an organization is often used as a barometer to gauge the performance and overall effectiveness of an organization. In the article "*Interpersonal Style and Corporate Climate: Communication Revisited*", Hall (1980) states in regard to the importance of communication:

> High on the diagnostic checklist of corporate health is communication. The ease with which information flows downward, upward, and horizontally is often a major internal indicant of organizational effectiveness; who listens to whom may reveal the real as opposed to the apparent authority structure in a firm; and the proportion of people who consistently fail to get the message is frequently taken as a statistical baseline for predicting the efficiency with which plans will be translated into actions.

This statement highlights the importance of effective communication in the workplace, and the potential negative ramifications of errant or misguided communication.

Communication is traditionally thought to have three main elements: a message, a sender, and a receiver. However, this is a stark over simplification of the process involved in workplace communications. Each of these stated elements has attached to it, several factors that must be considered in the process of communicating. The first to be analyzed here is the element of the message. Some of the more important considerations in regard to the message are: clarity, purpose, audience, meaning, complexity, and pertinence. Vague words or phrases may lead to ineffective results or no reaction at all from the intended recipient. Different words have different meanings to different people, depending on their age, economic status, position within the company, or cultural background.

The second element of communication is the sender, or source of the message. The sender must be known to, or have relevance to the recipient in order for the message to carry any importance in most cases. This element is closely related to the amount of communication an employee is subject to in the workplace. In many organizations, mass communications or cross-departmental communications are done every day that do not have particular relevance to everyone they are communicated to. This issue creates two problems; first, it increases the amount of information an employee is subject to and second, the information may not be pertinent to all those that read it. This situation has the effect of employees, over time, becoming immune to certain communications. It may also result in information overload, which may have an adverse effect on future employee communication. Employees generally prefer to hear from their direct supervisor, but in some cases, mass communication may be appropriate. As long as the sender of the information is legitimate, known, and relevant, employees will be more willing to internalize the message being sent.

The third element of communication is the receiver, which is closely related to the element of the sender in the regard that the receiver must be relevant and known. A relative message that is sent by a relevant sender, but is sent to an irrelevant recipient, has no effect and is wasted communication. If the receiver of the communication is relevant and is the intended audience, the message must be understandable to the employee. This concept goes back to the element of the message itself. If it contains information that is valuable and pertinent to the receiver, it will be received much better. Two important factors involved in the communication process that involve the receiver, and are used to ensure a successful communications loop, are follow-up and feedback. The sender should follow-up with the receiver to see whether or not the receiver has interpreted the meaning of the message as it was intended. To help facilitate this process, the receiver, in turn, should provide adequate feedback to the sender of the information that gives an indication that they received the information and understand its intended meaning. This process helps to close the continuous communications loop and ensure that the communication process was successful and effective.

This next section will consider communications in the traditional work environment, expectations of employees, and management's responsibility in regard to effective communication to employees. Many supervisors and managers already know and understand how important it is to be effective communicator's with employees. Communications in the workplace is not just about communicating directives; it is also concerned with building relationships, instilling trust, promoting mutual understanding, and providing a tool for employee involvement. Like many facets of an employee's job, communication can be taught, and effective organizations ensure that it is. In most cases, the communication style of an organization conveys the values and culture of that organization. Communication is not only an important part of each internal department, it is affected and shaped by the culture of a workplace and therefore demonstrates and transmits the characteristics of a workplace culture. Communication patterns within an organization typically follow the hierarchal model that exists, such as a command and control management style. If an organization's management exhibits an open, participative environment that is receptive to employee involvement, so too will be the communication style of the overall organization (Communication strategy, 2006).

Just like the planned direction of a company, so too should organizational communications have a strategy that is conveyed and understood by all members of the organization. Many organizations fail to recognize the importance of highlighting internal communications, but rather choose to assume that employees should automatically march in lock step with organizational priorities, strategies and initiatives. Companies that focus on improving the effectiveness of their internal communications experience increased productivity, customer centricity, employee satisfaction, and market value. Communication in progressive organizations reflects a view of the relationship with its workers. Management provides information to support participation of the workforce in decision-making. Collaborative employee-management communication is designed for the management and employees of an organization to mutually understand the strategies, goals, and initiatives that exist. It also allows all of the parties involved in these goals and initiatives to understand their roles, as well as expectations, in relation to meeting the objectives to be attained (Wilkins, 1989).

The goal of communication should be to facilitate the bilateral flow of information that should improve the employees' commitment to the organization's goals and objectives. Leadership must also be open to feedback. Employees need to believe they have a voice in the company and that their input matters. The management of an organization must do more than talk about bilateral communication; they must prove that it exists within the organization (Varelas, 2005). If employees see that the management of an organization is committed to a communications process that is based on respect, dignity, trust, and shared ideas, they will participate in the communications process openly and honestly.

An organization should have a strategy for internal communications, and that strategy should be shared with all employees. Organizations should delineate the communications expectations to employees and establish clear guidelines for communicating in the workplace. The communications strategy should be developed in order to encourage open two-way communication and also facilitate the exchange of information necessary to conduct the customer centric change. Having a strategy in place and everyone in the organization understanding it, is good management and helps to promote effective relationships within the organization. Some of the early research on this topic by Blake and Mouton (1968) revealed that where management is effective and relationships are sound, there are fewer problems with communication. The starting point for developing internal organizational communication processes that build trust and credibility is to establish a set of working principles as the foundation.

The issue of communication in the workforce is one of great breadth and size that covers many different sub topics. Certain advances in technology have helped modern communication, but at the same time, have created other issues that must be considered when examining the communication process. One of the positives of the introduction of technology to the communications process is the ability to communicate with many employees quickly, without regard for geographic location. An issue that exists in communicating with employees electronically is that most senders of information expect that when a message has been sent, and subsequently received, that it has been understood as intended. Brown (1973) said:

> The complex of technical devices which have come to facilitate the process of communication in larger organizations tends to divert attention from the essential truth that effective communication is more a matter of minds than of machines.

It is very easy to get lost in the technological advances that are related to communication. However, it is important for organizations to concentrate on effective communication and not get distracted by the technology itself (Harshman and Harshman, 1999). Flaherty (1997) indicates that effective organizational communication plays a major role in employee satisfaction as well as creating customer centric culture. High performing organizations provide channels for upward communication and listen to what employees say. A common factor revealed at many high-performing customer centric organizations is the very effective channels of communication that exist from the employees up to management. In these organizations, employees feel that their messages are heard by management and quite often used in the decision making process (MacGregor, 2006). Employees have an intrinsic need to know that their input counts and that when they attempt to communicate with management, the message is received and understood. All staff, no matter their length of tenure should have frequent opportunities to clarify goals of their work and give and receive feedback about how they perform their jobs. It does not matter what the content of the message may be, as long as workers feel that they can effectively and openly communicate with the management of the organization (Communications Strategy, 2006).

3.2.5 Teamwork

Only motivated and committed workers can successfully assist their organization to achieve its customer centric goals. Working smarter can only be achieved with an involved workforce. Teamwork has been proven to improve many of the factors related to employee satisfaction that includes increased motivation and productivity (Hamel, 1994). Teamwork is now being used as a behavioral modification tool, used to increase employee satisfaction and motivate groups of employees toward organizational goals and objectives (Morley and Heraty, 1995). The assumption behind teamwork is to upgrade autonomy that is realized in terms of identifying the best way of practicing a job to achieve the highest performance through continuous search of employees for alternative ways of work practices. Increased autonomy is expected to foster self-fulfillment and make jobs significant (Ross, 1999). Teamwork is often viewed as an efficient and motivating method of coordinating and condensing the individual contributions of individuals into one cohesive outcome. In this regard, teamwork is viewed as a motivational tool for the purpose of enhancing individual input and involvement through a group of employees working together in team environments (Rodwell et al., 1998).

Teamwork is not a new concept. The concept of "teams" has tended to be relegated to sports and media, rather than in business environments (Wellins et al., 1991). The sports analogy is often used to cite the benefits of teamwork in organizations. The idea being that a true team is a group of cohesive equals with a common goal. The team functions as an organic whole where the group truly is greater than the sum of its parts. The term "self-directed work teams" has been used since the 1950s to describe teams of employees working together toward one common goal. There is no universally accepted way of designing one of these teams because the formation process should be participative, and will probably differ from organization to organization. In the "typical" work environment, a *self-directed work team* is an intact group of employees who are responsible for a "whole" work process or segment that delivers a product or service to an internal or external customer. In essence, individuals work as an autonomous team that plan and control their work in order to achieve specified organizational goals and objectives (Wellins et al., 1991).

Extensive research in the field of employee satisfaction has supported the hypothesis that employees derive pleasure and satisfaction from socializing with their co-workers, with the greatest source of satisfaction coming as a member of an "on the job" team. That is a tremendous source of morale for employees. In fact, a good deal of the interaction while socializing is work related. Teamwork contributes to an environment of socializing between employees, in regard to work matters as well as non-work related matters. This socializing contributes to a solidifying of relationships between employees. This social interaction and team environment leads to the establishment of an effective and cohesive work community (Sirota et al., 2005). Although teamwork has been shown to improve employee satisfaction and worker productivity, it is often not managed well or even promoted by some organizations. Teamwork requires dedication and attention from management in order to be an effective morale and production tool. Teamwork is an important factor to manage well. Teamwork requires constant managerial attention and knowledge of the important elements associated with effective teamwork. Managers should understand the personalities involved in teams, the forming process, and the factors associated with successful team formation (Special, 2006).

Several researchers have found that employees realize greater job satisfaction and autonomy when able to work in teams (Ascigil, 2003). Therefore, an organization that promotes and encourages teamwork, and that provides an environment receptive to teamwork, stands to improve both employee satisfaction and productivity. It is claimed that the experiences of employees about team-based initiatives are shaped by multiple factors. Organizational behavior research has shown that management practices give rise to particular job attitudes on the part of employees. It has been found that the participation associated with teamwork leads to positive effects on job satisfaction and to the commitment level of employees (Boshoff and Mels, 1995).

Thus far, this section has focused on the positive attributes and benefits that stem from effective teamwork in an organization. There are however, negative effects of ineffective teamwork, or dissatisfied members of a team. When a member of the team experiences problems or worse yet, causes problems for other members of the team, the affected employee is not the only one that suffers. In fact, the issue may result in a breakdown of team cohesiveness and productivity. In fighting by team members cannot only cause team ineffectiveness, but also lead to individual mistrust and paranoia (Sirota et al., 2005). Because teams are a composition of individuals, they present many unique problems that must be addressed in a timely manner by management, as well as by the team members themselves. Quite often teams experience problems during the formation and forming stages of team development. Going in circles is a perfectly natural evolutionary stage and one that is important for the development of the group. Teams must go through different stages of formation in order to achieve autonomy as a group element. It is necessary for teams to experience tension and conflict on its way to becoming an effective entity. Groups that recognize and deal with conflict early on are much better equipped to handle issues that may arise later in the process (Wellins et al., 1991).

In addition to the employee satisfaction benefits that an organization is able to reap as a result of effective teamwork, there are other tangible benefits as well. These include employee empowerment, trust in management, and an engendered feeling of organizational involvement. Employee involvement practices have been one of the techniques extensively used for creating customer centric culture by pioneering organizations. Among those initiatives, redesign of work combined with job enrichment are two that are widely aiming at quality increases by creating jobs that entail autonomy and feedback. All of which are accomplished by effectively employing a teamwork strategy (Hackman and Oldham, 1980). As was previously stated, management has an important role in ensuring the success and intended outcome of teamwork in the organization. Management needs to fully understand the teamwork concept and realize that unless management behaves differently, nothing will change. Management needs to give the work-teams clear direction on what needs to be accomplished and autonomy and control over how they do the tasks. With the proper guidance, team members learn to act more like managers that are part of a larger organizational focus. Both management and the employees in the team can learn from the teaming process while contributing to the accomplishment of organizational objectives (Wellins et al., 1991).

3.2.6 Employee Empowerment

Empowerment in the workplace is an often-misunderstood concept. Employee empowerment is a term that many managers and organizations think they understand, but few actually do, and even fewer really put into practice. Many managers feel that by empowering employees, they relinquish the responsibility to lead and control the organization. This is not the case. Empowerment is actually a culmination of many of the ideas and tenets of employee satisfaction that have been discussed previously in this research. For an organization to practice and foster employee empowerment, the management must trust and communicate with employees (see Figure 3.4). The single most important element of employee empowerment is communication. Consistent communication from management in regard to every facet of the organization empowers the workforce and engenders a feeling in them as active participants in the success of the company (Adams, 2006). Employee empowerment has been described and defined in many ways but is generally accepted as: the process of enabling an employee to think, behave, act, react, and control their work in more autonomous ways, as to be in control of one's own destiny. Effective employee empowerment not only has positive implications for employee satisfaction, but also many other organizational facets, such as customer service and retention. This section will consider the implications of employee empowerment in creating a customer centric organization.

A great deal of managerial discussion has centered on the need to empower employees and give them a sense of ownership and pride in their work. Options have included flattening organizational pyramids and using team management. Many companies actually set out to increase employee empowerment by attempting to increase the level of entrepreneurship within the company (Denton, 2004). Traditionally, entrepreneurship has been thought of as a concept of independence and self-direction, a concept

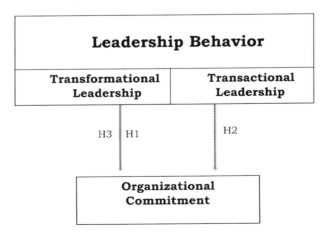

Figure 3.4   Leadership for Empowerment (Nova Southeastern University).

that is diametrically opposed to the process of a synergistic organization. However, the concept of entrepreneurship has been employed in successful organizations and is often referred to as "corporate entrepreneurship." Corporate entrepreneurship focuses on ways to encourage entrepreneurial activities in corporations, and seeks to identify relevant factors associated with corporations that exhibit characteristics most often associated with the individual entrepreneur (Gartner, 1988). The concept of corporate entrepreneurship is becoming more important to organizations everywhere as the need increases to retain good employees, while at the same time needing to constantly compete and innovate. Empowerment and entrepreneurship can be synonymous terms when trying to prompt employees to operate with more autonomy, take action, and ultimately control their own destiny. This motivational action often leads to employees feeling more independent and in control of their work situation, which in turn, is translated into greater effort and improved work productivity (Miecevole, 2006).

The most important factor in effective employee empowerment is bilateral communication. As previously mentioned, a key to employee empowerment is effective and honest communication. It requires that management increase the amount of time they devote to actively communicating with employees, as well as how they go about doing it (Hildula, 1996). Communicating and sharing information accomplishes several objectives that are not only important for the empowerment process, but also for overall employee satisfaction with the organization. The sharing of information lets people understand the current organizational situation in clear terms. It begins to build trust throughout the organization and breaks down traditional hierarchical thinking. Information leads to employees accepting more responsibility, making informed decisions, and having an understanding of the goals and objectives of the organization. Information ultimately empowers employees to act as stakeholders of the organization (Blanchard, 1996).

It is also important to remember that communication must work both ways. That is to say, employees must be allowed to have a say in issues that they are required to work with. This includes the opportunity to offer ideas and solutions to situations that may confront the organization. An important factor to consider when discussing idea generation is the treatment of the people involved in the process. It is vital that the participants receive feedback and feel that they have ownership in the process. People must know that their ideas will be listened to and, if they have merit, acted upon. If they do, it is possible to mobilize individual creativity on a very broad scale (Champy, 1995). Making sure the participants are treated fairly and as equal partners in the process is a key to successful innovation and creativity.

Everyone involved in the process must believe that anything is possible and that exploring new paradigms and ways of thinking are the goals. Fear of failure and retribution for unsuccessful ventures cannot be presented as impediments to the process. Punishing the innovator when an innovation fails is the best way to ensure that no one ever attempts to be innovative (Hammer and Champy, 1993). One last note about the people involved in the process is in regard to the hiring of the people themselves. Far too often we hire people in our own image. By doing this, we inadvertently create a uniform, standard line of thinking and methodology. The most efficient way to introduce creativity and innovation into an organization is by hiring creative and innovative people. In order to effectively do this, the leadership of an organization must be willing to step outside of their comfort zone and hire people that may be different from themselves (Freiberg, 2005).

Employee empowerment requires a strong and lasting commitment from an organization's management. A pervasive misconception in relation to employee empowerment is that it is a top down desire. Employee empowerment comes from the individual. That is not to say that management ceases to have the responsibility to lead the group and is not responsible for performance. In fact, companies that seek to empower employees demand stronger leadership and accountability. This strong leadership and accountability must start at the very top and permeate all levels of management. Once the organization becomes a cohesive, understanding team, the real benefits of employee empowerment can then be realized (Butcher, 2006). It is up to the management of an organization to lead the empowerment process, even though it is most likely the employees that are advocating the issue. Creating and stimulating employee empowerment in established organizations is not an expeditious proposition. It is an easier proposition in newer organizations where the leadership has made empowerment of its employees a priority from the beginning. For this reason, it is incumbent on the leadership of established organizations to demonstrate the benefits and expected outcomes of employee motivation initiatives to employees (Fox, 1998).

A good lens by which to examine the employee and organizational benefits of employee empowerment is through the customers of the organization. It is a well-known fact that companies who are truly successful customer centric have several traits in common, one of which is employee empowerment. This empowerment is exhibited by employees that are able to make on the spot decisions for the benefit of customer service delivery (Haley, 2006; Rampersad, 2009). There are now many companies that tout employee empowerment as a selling point to prospective customers. They advertise the fact that the employee empowerment philosophy allows their employees several important capabilities, including the ability to respond intelligently and independently to customer needs, and make critical decisions on-the-spot. Because employee empowerment leads to more satisfied and motivated employees, organizations are able to deliver higher quality, lasting customer service (Catapult, 2007). Since our society has become a "service" related society, with a service-based economy, empowering employees to make customer service related decisions is imperative to organizational success towards the customer centric principals. It is necessary for customer service employees to exercise a higher level of personal judgment than their manufacturing counterparts because of their proximity to the customer service delivery experience (Huq and Stole, 1998). Using this reasoning, one can easily see that empowering employees to make customer service related decisions will result in the satisfaction of the customer, employee, and subsequently, the organization.

In addition to the employee, organizational and customer benefits already cited here, employee empowerment holds added benefits and outcomes for employees. One of the measures of success for any organization is the personal growth and development of its employees. Empowerment allows employees the opportunity to build on their current skill set. Being empowered gives them the ability to use all the skills that they already possess as well as gain new skills and experiences. Being able to practice these skills and exercise their creativity and innovation will help them improve upon future performance (Hayes, 2003). When encouraged and managed properly, empowerment can be a great solution for many organizational problems. Once organizations and employees are able to understand and practice employee empowerment, they can then begin to recognize personal and corporate growth that results from the empowerment initiative (Butcher, 2006).

3.2.7 *Employee Motivation*

The theory of motivation is really rooted in the field of psychology. Because of this, one can infer that motivation is unique to the particular individual, affected by different circumstances. Motivation is the set of processes that moves a person toward a goal. The purpose of behavior is to satisfy needs. A need is anything that is required, desired, or useful. A want is a conscious recognition of a need. A need arises when there is a difference in self-concept (the way I see myself) and perception (the way I see the world around me) (Allen, 1998). Although there are several cited motivation theories, two of the more popular will be discussed here: Maslow's Hierarchy of Needs, and Herzberg's Two-Factor Theory (see Figure 3.5). Work motivation is one of the key areas of organizational psychology. Using

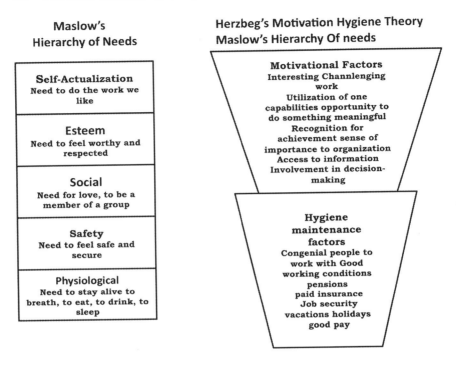

Figure 3.5 Motivational Theories (Allen, 1998).

these two different motivational theories, this paper will analyze the motivation triggers used to maximize employee motivation and satisfaction which contribute to create a customer centric culture.

Frederick Herzberg developed a two-factor theory of motivation that makes clear what the employer can bring to the motivation partnership. According to Herzberg, two factors affect employee motivation: dissatisfiers (sometimes referred to as Hygiene) and motivators. While at work, the organization is in control of both factors. Dissatisfaction (hygiene) or extrinsic factors, excessive hours, unsafe working conditions, job security, and low wages, produce job dissatisfaction. Motivator or intrinsic factors, such as increased responsibility, adequate training and development opportunities, recognition, and satisfying work, produce job satisfaction (see Figure 3.6).

The implications for the employer's side of the motivation partnership are clear. The dissatisfiers must be removed before motivators can work. Employees working in unsafe conditions with unfair pay will not be motivated by recognition and delegation of additional responsibility. However, if improvements in both safety and pay are made, employees may still not

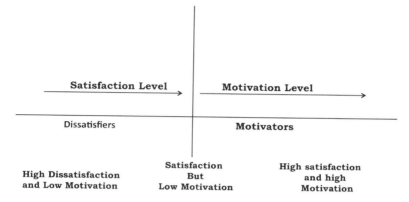

Figure 3.6 Motivation and Satisfaction Levels (Ohio State University).

become motivated. Instead, if all else remains the same the employees will become satisfied but not motivated (Erven and Milliganm, 2001).

The second of the two psychological theories of motivation, and probably the most widely recognized, was first introduced by Abraham Maslow and is known as Maslow's Hierarchy of Needs.

Maslow's Hierarchy of Needs identifies five levels of needs, which are best seen as a hierarchy with the most basic need emerging first and the most sophisticated need last (see Figure 3.7). People move up the hierarchy one level at a time. Gratified needs lose their strength and the next level

Figure 3.7 Maslow's Hierarchy of Needs (Allen, 1998).

of needs is activated. As basic or lower-level needs are satisfied, higher level needs become operative. Therefore, a satisfied need is not a motivator (Allen, 1998). The basic human needs, according to Maslow are: physiological needs (lowest), safety needs, love needs, esteem needs, and self-actualization needs (highest). This theory indicates that man's behavior is therefore dominated by his unsatisfied needs. As each need is satisfied, another is created, making the cycle a perpetual, ongoing activity of searching for perfection through self-development (Accel, 2006).

Motivating employees is a constant task that requires an understanding of employee psychology, as well as an understanding of individual motivators. The key to motivation unlocks human potential. To be effective, managers need to understand what motivates employees within the context of the roles they perform. Of all the functions a manager performs, employee motivation is one of the most complex management issues they face. As employees find an outlet for their creativity and satisfaction with their work, the work they perform becomes a more important part of their life. As a result, employees become more productive and experience higher rates of satisfaction with their employment (Erven and Milligan, 2001; Rampersad, 2014). In the past, managers assumed incorrectly, that all it would take to motivate employees is to pay them more. It is conceivable for an organization to have more employees than a competitor yet produce less and have disgruntled, low-output employees even though the organization is paying their employees more than the competitor. Organizations are beginning to understand that they are able to motivate increased productivity and employee satisfaction by means other than financial incentives (Increasing Productivity, 2005).

The foundation of good human relations, the interaction between employer and employees and their attitudes toward one another, is a satisfied work force. Job satisfaction is the degree of enjoyment that people derive from performing their jobs. Satisfied and motivated employees are more likely to have high morale, loyalty and commitment. As a result, they tend to be more dedicated and make larger contributions to the initiatives and goals of the organization (Allen, 1998). An organization's level of understanding of how to motivate its employees can be considered directly related to the level of productivity and employee satisfaction realized at the organization.

3.2.8 Fair Treatment of Employees

The customer-centric organization depends not only on furnishing employees with an amiable workplace, but also a fair workplace. It is important not to discriminate among employees, employing different standards to different individuals or groups of workers. Fairness is especially important when it comes to considerations of pay and promotion. In seeking to keep its staff contented, a company must make certain that equitable standards are applied across the board. Special programs must not be instituted that favor one class of employee with stilted pay scales or incentives that are simply not available to others. Some organizations actively implement just these sorts of programs as a means of encouraging people to join the company. College students might be given incentives to sign with an organization after they graduate, or perhaps, to seek summer employment. Workers might be sought for a new department or division and these workers lured to the organization by promises of extra benefits or extra-rapid advancement: Now the practice is used for new college graduates and hard-to fill technical and customer service jobs. Every time we add a pay practice that makes economic sense for one group of employees, we are perceived to put other employees at a disadvantage. Employees who thought that their pay was okay become dissatisfied with it when they learn about opportunities for pay that they cannot share in. Having a variety of reasons for paying employees inevitably creates invidious comparisons. After a while we find ourselves with a number of pay practices that do not seem to work for us. Accoding to the work by Suzanne (1999), they:

- Have conflicting goals.
- Are hard to administer.
- Increase labor costs more than we think they should.
- Are not consistent with our mission and values.
- Confuse employees.
- Cause morale problems between the haves and have-nots.

Again, these distinctions among employees lead to loss of service for customers. If they are not treated fairly themselves, personnel see no reason to devote themselves to company goals, and therefore, no particular reason to go that extra mile in providing excellent service or, indeed, doing anything to ensure that customers are retained or the customer base is expanded.

One idea is for the customer-centric organization to employ its workforce in observational capacity. Workers actually get to recommend what constitutes best practice in customer service (Jack, Scott, & Kyle, 2006). The concept makes perfect sense as the employees themselves are closest to those they serve. The policy also builds employee self-esteem and further increases levels of custom service by making employees feel they are a part of the solution, and that their thoughts and actions are appreciated by the company. Study shows a correlation of .32 percent for service excellence and .17 for employee satisfaction when the organization chooses to emphasize a customer-centric approach (Jack, Scott, & Kyle, 2006). Flexibility in workplace arrangements also helps to retain valuable employees and to foster an atmosphere of opportunity and equity. All workers can be offered such things as flexible work schedules, telecommuting, and similar options. Two different studies reveal the importance of these offerings, one showing fifty-three percent of employees considering telecommuting an important option, while in another twenty-three percent report that they would quit their jobs if they could not telecommute (Brandi, 2001). Southwest Airlines offers an example in which a large company places a premium on employee empowerment. In this instance, the company de-emphasizes the corporate hierarchy and instead plays up teamwork and employee independence; even encouraging employees to work in unsupervised locations where they will have the responsibility to make their own customer service decisions. And in yet another study cited by Subhash and Jay (2004), the link is explicitly made between a quality, well-managed workforce, and the maintenance of a high level of success in each of the following five areas of customer service:

- Reliability: Ability to deliver services as promised
- Responsiveness: Willingness to provide prompt service and help customers
- Assurance: Ability to communicate credibility and to convey trust and confidence
- Empathy: Willingness to provide caring and individualized attention to customers
- Tangibles: Maintaining the appearance of physical facilities and personnel

And in three further studies cited by Michael, Kevin and Henry (2004), autonomy and power distance are shown to be significant factors in job satisfaction all over the world. Employees feel better about themselves and the work that they do if they feel that they are given genuine responsibility to make their own decisions. Furthermore, freedom of action is valued in the sense that workers perform better if they do not feel they occupy grossly inferior positions to managers and supervisors *i.e.*, power distance. This is still another example of the importance of teams and teamwork in promoting a sense of camaraderie within the workplace. Such camaraderie actually promotes individual contentment among workers. Employee involvement is an essential element in capturing market share, and increasing innovation and productivity (Bonnie and Teresa, 2000). Each of these elements contributes directly to customer centricity.

4

Corporate Centricity

The second stage in the authentic customer centricity journey is primarily concerned with corporate centricity (see Figure 4.1).

4.1 Organizational Barriers

Customer centric companies focus on the processes and technology that support and enhance a customer centric strategy. They realized that process and technology changes are the corner stone of becoming a truly customer centric organization. The true essence of the customer centricity paradigm lies not in how to sell services or products but rather on creating value from both the customer and the company, in other words customer centricity is related to the process of dual value creation. A customer centric organization prices its offering on the basis of the value it creates to customers not on the basis of market condition (Jay, 2005).

In this context it is important to integrate customer centricity strategy, organizational processes, structure and information technology so that the whole organization will move towards customer centricity. Customer

---

Authentic Customer Centricity, pages 43–63
Copyright © 2015 by Information Age Publishing
All rights of reproduction in any form reserved.

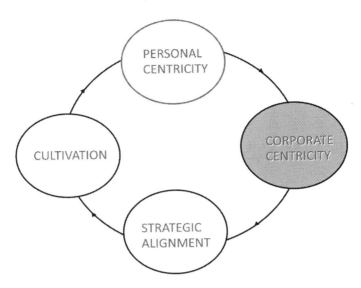

Figure 4.1 Second Stage in the Authentic Customer Centricity Model.

centricity is the ultimate state of the customer being in full control of the buying process. Being customer centric means that the customers say what they buy, how it is delivered, designed and packaged and how much they should pay and when they pay (David, 2007). Customer service tends to be a generic and determined in advance for its customers whereas customer centric is about providing a personalized service to individual customers. It is a statement of intent. It signals the organization is willing to challenge the status silo and embrace new concepts and management disciplines. Such a commitment is evidence that the transition to customer focus is an evolutionary process that requires the organization structure, culture and business processes to be structured and continually restructured to respond to individual customer needs.

At the center of this is the customer. All too often organizations assume they know what their customers want. This is a dangerous and naïve assumption and will only serve to lessen the degree of fit between what the organization offers and what the customers want. It is very necessary that companies focus on the customers and attempt to get close to them, their needs, share their concerns and develop future needs. The process of identifying customers must be well disciplined and adhered to. The customer needs to be rigorously studied from bottom of the organization right to the very top. Such a commitment necessitates a change in all three aspects of

Customers

Figure 4.2 Customer Reach (John, 2006).

organization namely, corporate culture, process and organization structure. These concepts are going to be discussed separately later in this section.

John (2006) has identified clearly that there are six layers that stand between the organization and their customers. These barriers create a challenge to companies to become customer centric. The barriers both connect and separate the organization from the customers. Figure 4.2 presents these barriers in the form of a hierarchy where the valued assets sits at the top and the many hoped-for customers sit at the bottom.

To make a real change in any organization, companies have to invert the pyramid shown in Figure 4.2, connect the customer psyche intimately with the asset of the organization as shown in Figure 4.3.

Once the organizations are able to make this challenge happens by putting the customer at the center of all the operations within the company, they will discover that customers are more inspired and loyalty has increased. The company profitability will be enhanced and the customer centric model starts rolling out.

The real challenge facing companies is building a customer centric organization. For example, a telecom company should move to a communication provider, a relaxed company to a vibrant competitor, a sole provider to a brand of choice, a place of work to the place to work, and from a work force to a community. Figure 4.4 shows this path to customer centricity.

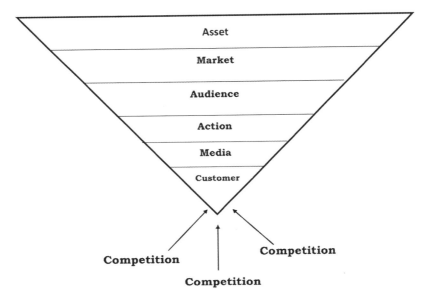

Figure 4.3 Inverted Figure 4.2 (John, 2006).

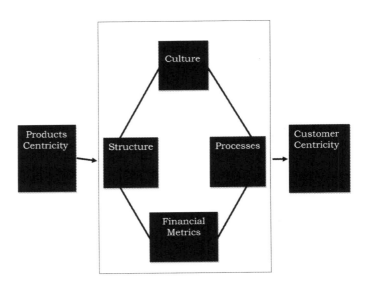

Figure 4.4 Path to Customer Centricity (Denish et al., 2006)

4.2 Organization Culture

According to Wilson (1997), corporate culture comprises visible and less visible norms, values and behavior that are shared by a group of employees which shape the groups sense of what is acceptable and what is valid. These are generally slow to change and new group members learn them through a formal and informal socialization process. Consequently program of change will be complicated and long term. The transition to a customer centric culture necessitates change in practices and procedures that facilitate the delivery of services. Craig (2006) adds that the key to succeed in moving toward customer centricity culture is to constantly change the business model based on a more detailed understanding of the target audience, customers and employees are one of the most important success key drivers.

Cultures have many levels and facets, which make them very resistance to change. Denish (2006) stated that values which express enduring preferences and behavioral attitudes of the front line employees are considered to be one of the difficult barriers to overcome toward the customer centricity path. He added that norms, which are shared beliefs about preferable or expected behavior. Customer centered organization is that employees are customer advocates. Sharing information among the members of the organization is a common norm of customers centered companies; this will put the company in a better position to understand and meet the needs of the customers. Conversely Sarah (2002) pointed out that a destructive norm found in many firms is that sales own the customer which greatly impedes information sharing. And Craig (2006) states that a leader should share as much information as is practically possible. Everyone is on the same team, right? If so, everyone needs abundant information about the direction and performance of the organization especially in relation to satisfying customers.

Denish et al. (2006) and Craig (2006) have stated that customer centric organizations are characterized by two main factors, the behavior of senior managers and employees exhibit as they make choices about how to spend their time. Time spent among the customers is a clear indication of the solid commitment of both leaders and employees toward customer centricity approach. So, it clear that senior management must reinforce and monitor the customer centric values that company strategy is driving, and it is imperative that they should buy in and commit to those values.

Overall, culture can be either an important facilitator of performance or a major impediment. When Deshpande et al. (1993) compared four types of organizational cultures based on the degree of emphasis on customers, they found that market cultures that place the customers' interest first were the most profitable and successful cultures.

Employees must be made aware of the benefits and implications of adopting a market culture that leads to customer centric organization. They need to be clear of the organization objectives and reasons for change. They must possess a fluent understanding of the organizations' agenda, their role in attaining this and what is expected of them and the senior management needs to articulate this in such a way that it energizes employees about helping customers. In order to accept and support this shared vision it is important for senior management to empower employees to take action on behalf of customers. Empowerment releases employee's judgment, initiative and creativity in serving customer requirements and loyalty (Scheuing, 1999). Similarly, Sarah (2002) stated that giving people responsibility for decisions affecting their work encourages a customer centric approach.

Cultural change is achieved by altering behavior patterns and helping employees to be trained in customer focused behavior. It must be ingrained that customer satisfaction is the central concern of the whole organization and everyone is responsible and accountable for delighting customers. People are a critical factor to achieve customer centric culture.

4.3 Organizational Structure

One way of understanding the organizational structure is to consider its function and purpose. As Newman (1973) describes, its meaning is to hold the things together, to give it form rather than randomness, to give it consistency and stability, to relate its parts to one another, and to delineate its operations. He also recognizes some general aspects that lead to the need for a structure. As far as the organization's tasks concern, it is desirable to allocate what activities that are needed and who will perform them and as well as knowing what decisions that has to be made and the resources necessary for activities. Structure will also clarify the co-workers relation to each other and what they should have. This reasoning also implies that, structure follows strategy. However, there are critics indicating that it yet can be the other way around; that structure needs to be set out first and strategy becomes a product of the structural forces (Booz Allen Hamilton, 2004). However, structure is there to straighten out people's role, responsibilities and authority, consequently contributing to an overall organizational understanding, for co-workers as well as parties with external interests. A clear organizational structure, where co-workers easily understand their area of responsibility and how their actions affect the overall business performance is important. It facilitates contribution of values to the customer value process as a whole. Further, it creates a broader responsibility, higher overall understanding of the organization, higher motivation and engagement (Amerup-Cooper & Edvardsson, 1998).

According to Mintzberg (1989) you can strive for and clench on to internal consistency of organization structure variables but at the cost of bad fit to the external environment and that finally forces a change in term of complete structural redesign. The way the organization appears might not depend so much on what the market forces looks like as on culture and institutionalization aspects. Thus, such possible barriers must be taken into account when imposing change on an organization (Homburg, et al., 1999). If an organization is designed to complete a certain task, then the reason for success or failure lays in the fit to its basic purpose. Natural structures exist in all organizations and there is a strong need for synchronization among parts within it. A fatally wrong assumption is that every organization looks the same, and as a consequence, the structure of an organization is inserted or extracted as picked randomly up from a shop. Thus there are implications that the recipe for organizational success in design is to be consistent and logical in defining their structural dimensions. Such dimensions are, for instance, various degrees of centralization, formalization and specialization (Mintzberg, 1989). Mintzberg is not alone in having studied the structure dimensions of organizations. There are many answers to the question of what the dimensions of structure really are. Common responses concur with Mintzberg and are for instance formalization, centralization, complexity and span of control (Blackburn, 1982) and (Olsen et al., 2005). However, I will stick to Mintzberg's dimensions of the organization structure in general: formalization, centralization and specialization and will link this definition to the customer centricity structure.

An ideal customer centric organization structure implies having all functional activities integrated and aligned to deliver superior customer value. Such an organization can provide a 360 degree customer perspective with necessary insights and foresights. This is in contrast to the product centric structure which is organized around functional silos generally lacking the necessary link between products and customer patterns (Day, 1999). Organizational structure of customer focused companies must be developed and flattened to enable a smooth coordination of customer direct processes. The customer must be the catalyst for reengineering of processes (Scheuing, 1999). Denish, et al. (2006) stated that there is mounting evidence that organization structures are evolving toward closer alignment with market conditions, especially from firms that want to have a consistent and seamless transactions in all of its touch points. They continued explaining this type of alignment through two stages; the first one is the emergence of informal coordination activities that serve to overcome the familiar deficiencies of functional silos. If this is not sufficient the second stage is going to be integrating functions such as key account managers to coordinate all customer contact activities.

Booz Allen (2004) has raised a very important point towards the journey to customer centricity; to strengthen operating economics and business unit linkage, telecommunications service providers will need to change the way they are organized to do business. It means that organization levers from structure to management systems to processes and to roles and responsibilities will need to be changed, even overhauled. The challenge of moving a company from product centric to a customer centric is explained by Denish et al. (2006). The challenge arises from the fact that functional differences are deeply rooted in background and interest, time scales, incentives and interests. Hence, any effort toward this subject is going to be related to the improvement of alignment of the organization which is subjected to contending forces.

4.4 Processes and Procedures

We ought to start off with the definition of a business process. Sometimes the term business process is used to talk about high-level descriptions of organization's activities which are used to describe market-oriented aspects like the satisfaction of customer needs (Olaf and Frank, 2000). The business process comprises all activities carried out in an enterprise, including e. g. staffing, financing, production, marketing, etc. Figure 4.5 shows a rather general model of business processes. In general, business process comprises activities that produce an output of value to the customer. A business process can be thought of as a box turning a certain input into an

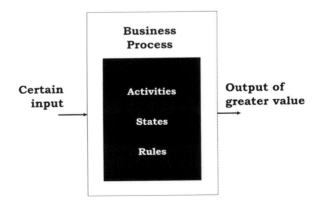

Figure 4.5   The General Model of Business Processes (Michael, 1997).

output of greater value (Michael, 1997). Usually it is the desired output of the customer but it can also add value to the company itself.

The business process of product development, for instance, has an idea or concept as an input and gets a design of prototype as an output. In order to get the desired output, many kinds of people have to participate, such as, research and development departments (contributing their technical expertise), marketing (offer knowledge of customers' needs), manufacturing experts and finance people. The process activities are the means to transform the input into the desired output. At any time the activities have a specific state and the process glow is determined by business rules. In other words, a business process can be thought of as a cook book for running a business.

History showed us the importance of business processes. In the 1980s the inefficiencies and in accuracies of company performances were beginning to matter. Before, customers had much choice where to buy specific product, but in the 1980s customers started deserting to other companies when they were not satisfied because they had simply the choice due to increasing competition. At that time many corporations had to improve their business to keep their customers. After attempts to change their situation, they found out the main problem. It was the fact that they were applying task solutions to process problems. A task is a unit of work usually performed by one person. In contrast, a process comprises of tasks and activities to create a result of value to the customer (Michael, 1997). That was the time when organizations got aware of the importance of business processes. It is vital for their survival to let them be at the heart of the company. In other words, clear business processes and procedures are the key to a successful customer centric organization. This is probably the case as they focus on creating value for customers.

To implement a customer centric business strategy, the organization must have better processes and procedures standards. Effective business process, innovation and responsiveness in the changing complex environment are very important for achieving business success and competitive advantage. The organization has to manage the processes and procedures with application of knowledge, skills, techniques and systems to meet customer requirements and expectations (Icfi, 2007). Denish et al. (2006) stated the difference among customer product and customer centric companies. The customer centric organizations, their processes and procedures aimed to develop and sustain a customer relationship, while the product centric is aimed to achieve an efficient transaction regardless of the quality of relationship with customers.

Payne and Frow (2005) surveyed a number of customer relationship management (CRM) executives and indicated five generic processes that contribute heavily for the firm to be customer centric, namely;

a. The strategy – development process that not only includes a business strategy but also a customer strategy.
b. The dual creation process which considered to be of the exchange process. ????????????
c. The multi-channel integration process that encompasses all the customer touch points.
d. The information management process which includes the data collection and analysis functions.
e. The performance assessment process which ties the firm's action to firm actual performance. Day (1999) pointed out a very crucial challenge concerning customer centric companies that look to develop a business processes and seek to optimally match the customer's requirements with the right product/service. To achieve this, companies should segment their customers into different groups based on their different needs and expectations.

Recent advances in IT and marketing database have facilitated marketing personalization processes as increased dialogues with the customer, making use of these dialogues processes and analyzing the collected information to allow the firm to make more values offers. However, he stresses that firms should be careful in terms of the level of automation of services' delivery. For example, some banks made huge investments in IT to automate and standardize huge banking transactions only to find out that they were losing human interactions with their customers. By offering virtually all services online or through automated phone/ATM centers, many banks had unknowingly distanced themselves from their customers.

In the same vein, organizations need to know their customers as individuals, concentrate on serving those with highest needs and lifetime profitability potential. To achieve such dramatic shift in culture, the CEO needs to take the lead of customer strategies and the organization's culture and processes to make this happen in the ground. This is considered to be a major challenge facing organization to re-engineer the whole processes and procedures that are customer related to be aligned with the customers' needs and expectations, and built around customers' segmentation strategy.

Organizations which strive to achieve new strategic position in the market should concentrate on aligning their organization structure and business processes with their customers' needs. This needs to modify their internal processing architecture to reflect a market rather than a product centric approach (Raul et al., (2004).

Robert (2004) and Day (1999) have similar point view towards the challenge facing organization to align their processes and procedures with customer centricity approach as well as consumers' needs. Their approach is very relevant and coincides with its existing conditions. It is clear that there is an extensive agreement in the literature that aligning the cross functional processes and procedures is very crucial for the success of the long–way to customer centricity. Cross–functional integration and synchronization is therefore a key success factor in coming up with pragmatic and sound customer centric strategy across the organization and to ensure that every function is aligned with the strategic move towards the customer focus company.

4.5 Operational and Financial Metrics

Customer centricity metrics such as operational and financial measures are not only important in motivating individual employees to be more customer centric, they are also useful in helping management at organizations to the financial and operational implications of their decision making and to think of marketing and sales expenditures as investments (Srivastavam et al. 1998). This point is crucial because the journey towards customer centricity demand a substantial investment by the company to move from a product centric to customer centric. Hence, the need to monitor, control and measure the operational and financial impact of customer orientation (see Figure 4.6).

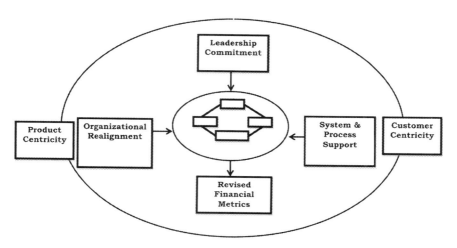

Figure 4.6 Path to Customer Centricity: Paving the Way (Denish et al., 2006).

A comprehensive approach to customer measures should be adopted as these serve as an important way of judging the overall success of organizations from the customers' perspective, provide a source of market information, provide a basis for setting goals and taking corrective action (Adebanjo & Kehoe, 2001). Measures may include satisfaction, complaints, product delivery, product return, customer requirements, sales figures, benchmarking of operational performance and response times to customer enquiries. Customer satisfaction should be a paramount goal of every employee and, although difficult to quantify, some measurement should be attempted. Measurements must be defined from the customer's perspective and standards developed such as response times, staff interface, reliability and service level thresholds.

Complaints are an invaluable source of information on where process breakdown therefore, a structured approach to complaints should be adopted. Reverting potential defectors and managing customer dissatisfaction will lead to an increase in customer satisfaction. The importance of this point is illustrated by figures suggested by Zairi (1999); satisfied customers share their experience with 5 or 6 people, yet dissatisfied customers share their experiences with 24 least to others.

Monitoring and tracking this transformation to customer centricity may not be an easy task. Devoting resources to a customer centric system is tantamount to investing in the construction of a virtual factory that generates intangible output such as customer satisfaction, loyalty, advocacy, reduced price sensitivity and so on (Hart, 1999). The intangible outputs may be difficult to measure directly. Hence, the challenge lies in quantifying the financial impact of customer centricity by determining the optimal levels of investment in such measures as customer satisfaction and loyalty.

Customer life time value (CLV) and its implications have received increasing attention (Berger and Nasr, 1998; Reinartz and Kumar, 2000). In the other side, Booz Allen (2004) shows that brand equity, a fundamentally product centric concept, has been challenged by the customer centered concept of customer equity. In addition tracking and measuring individual customer level value helps firms manage resources at the individual customer level, thereby making the financial and operational orientation of the firm compatible with its customer orientations. For example, customer equity has been shown to be reasonable proxy for firm implying that strategies that improve customer equity will also enhance the value of the firm value (Grupta, Lehamann and Stuart, 2004).

The application of customer equity as the focal point for guiding financial impact of marketing actions is apparent in its versatility. Spanning several applications and instances of managerial decision making for example, customer equity can be used as a basis for optimally allocating a firm's resources across customers (Yenkatesan and Kumar, 2004).

Another important issue related to both financial impact and the challenge of achieving customer centricity is downsizing – that is, cutting costs through reducing headcounts to enhance financial performance cost reduction programs, for example, downsizing customer service staff or outsourcing customer service to a cheaper offshore location to reduce cost and improve productivity. Transfer savings associated with these programs, directly to the bottom line look great on firm's annual reports. However, the apparent financial attractiveness of such cost cutting measures and consequent propensity to adopt them hastily are a potential impediment to achieving customer centricity. Decisions to downsize or outsource should be carefully evaluated as they may result in increased productivity in the short term but may threaten future profitability if customer satisfaction is highly dependent on the efforts of the downsized personnel or quality of the outsourced functions (Anderson, Fornell and Rust, 1997; Oliva and Steman, 2001). Furthermore, the implementation of a cost cutting emphasis, instead of revenue expansion emphasis, has the tendency to initiate unpleasant initiatives such as, firing and/or loss of benefits and perks which may lower the morale of employees who operate at the market interface. This in turn may lower customer service, customer loyalty and sales which lead to further cost cutting – a vicious circle or "death spiral" that may seriously affect the firm's performance in the long run and be a real barrier toward customer centricity. In summary, companies must adopt necessary operational and financial metrics as a pathway for building a customer centric organization to boost shareholder value. Performance review of an organization along these KPIS are critical for executing the strategy plan, and organizations need to constantly enhance customer life time value (CLTV) and Net Promoter Score (NPS) against competition.

4.6 Building a Customer Centric Organization

Becoming a customer centric or focused and driven organization requires more than just deciding that it is a good idea in order to boost sales and revenues. It requires dedication, time, commitment and a good deal of effort. In their quests to become customer centric organization firms must consider that it is not enough just to take care of the customer today, they must think beyond today and plan for what the customer will desire tomorrow. Organization must do more than anticipate customers' stated needs and become proficient at anticipating unarticulated needs and desires (Hamel and Prahalad, 1994). This is not always a necessary thing to do, especially when technology is involved. However, organizations that make the investment are required to change their whole way of thinking often find that the process is made easier. At the heart of becoming a true customer centric organization is the ability to create value for the customer whenever they come into contact with an organization. What drives this new model is not profit but the creation of value for the customer, a process that lies at the core of all successful enterprises. Value creation generates the energy that holds these businesses together and their very existence depends on it (Reichheld, 1996).

Organizations that become customer centric understand that their business is no longer about product or service that they once provided, it is now about the customer that uses the product or service provided by the organization. Customers don't buy products or services; they buy value. The attitude and quality of the service provided to customers play an important role (Heskett, Sasser, and Schlesinger 1997). Customer centric organizations ask questions differently. Their values, mission and organizational structures exist for the customer, not the organization or its owner.

A first step in the journey towards customer centricity is to define and understand what it means to the organization. The definition of customer centricity that I suggest is: Aligning resources of 'your organization' to effectively respond to the ever-changing needs of the customer, while building mutually positive relationship. Now, let's break that definition down into three parts so that we can discuss each of them.

1. Aligning organization resources.
2. Respond to the ever-changing needs of the customers effectively.
3. Building mutual profitable relationship.

Becoming a customer centric organization does not mean that organization becomes a door mat for the customer. If the relationship for both the customers and companies does not remain profitable, it is not going to last for long. Aligning the resources of organization is ensuring that all personnel in the firm develop and maintain excellent interpersonal communication skills. The last, not the least factor that contributes to build customer centric organization explained by Bailey (2006) is to effectively respond to the ever-changing needs of the customers. To do this, organizations need to obtain customer input, perspective and feedback in support of the voice of the customer. The tools that can be used to attain such requirement are; transactional surveys to measure customer's satisfaction, observe customer behavior, obtain input from front line employees and mystery shopping experience. Jay (2005) stated an example for a company called Chipco which is a product centric company, in the semiconductor industry. Chipco had gone through several re-structuring programs toward a customer centric organization; it adopted star model structure shown in Figure 4.7. The Chipco's solutions Star Model started with strategy and then completed the star model design by moving from strategy to structure to process to rewards to people. The strategy consists of product and service strategy plus selected solutions for selected segment of customers. The structure is combined of product division at the back end and business units and customer segments in the front line. Business processes have been added for solutions development, pricing and supply chain management. The reward system has been modified to reflect a one company down model. Finally the career paths for the Chipco's people have been redesigned to generate leaders for the new business unit. The overall re-structuring of this firm was led by the top management and communicates to every employee in the firm (Bailey, 2006).

Cristian (2006) in the other hand proposed an important basic step that a company must take in its efforts to become customer centric. He recommended three main steps in the journey of customer centricity, namely, employees' training, everybody should think in term of customer benefits rather than product features. Refine the organizational structure, which includes fine tuning the information channels, allowing knowledge about the customer to flow freely throughout the organization. The final step is

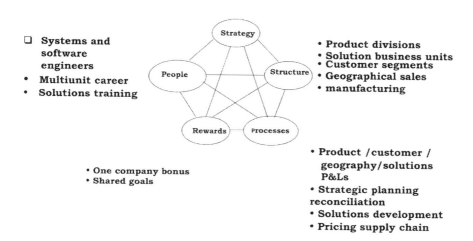

Figure 4.7 Chipco' Solutions Star Model (Jay, 2005).

to ensure the right market approach between the company products and services approach and customers' behavior.

Raul et al. (2004) frame work offers another perspective on building customer centric companies. According to his frame shown in Figure 4.8, there are design principles that telecommunications service providers should keep in mind during the designing phase of customer centric organization:

- Differentiate the customer experience through new, open and transparent approach.
- Redesign distribution and customer management around a solution approach.
- Develop a segmentation process that differentiates your customer based on needs.
- Pull away from competitors by getting execution right the first time.

Putting these four principals working together will yield to a vast transformation of the organizations.

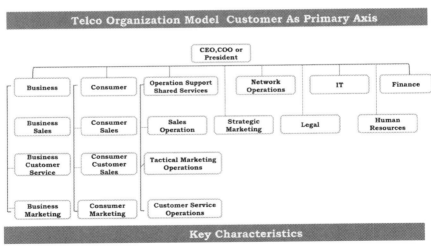

Figure 4.8 Customer Centric Operating Model for Telecommunications Provider (Raul et al., 2004).

These organizations are no longer organized around functional or product areas; instead, customer segments are the primary axis. Building a customer-centric organization, in our experience, requires repositioning the business around an optimized continuum of tailored solutions. To achieve these repositioning, telecom providers need to shift from a product-centric mindset to full service providers. The telecommunications company of the future will provide tailored bundles of products and services to anyone, anytime, anywhere, anyhow (Booz Allen Hamilton, 2004).

4.7 Customer Relationship Management

Given the complexities of customer relation, many companies have turned to innovative solutions that help them to achieve success in an increasingly competitive global marketplace. Computers are essential not only for the running of a company, but for virtually every aspect of the entire business paradigm. Computer programs help with the many components that come together to create a high level of customer satisfaction. The computer systems themselves reflect the many individual areas with which the customer centric organization must concern itself. As stated above many areas of customer satisfaction and employee satisfaction overlap. This brings into the picture the many business features that profoundly affect customer satisfaction. Among these are human resources and its subsets of employee compensation and benefits management. Also included under the operational concerns that affect customer satisfaction, are the various decision-making capabilities of management i.e., business intelligence, supply chain, planning, marketing, and so forth. Nearly everything to do with a modern day business somehow affects the end customer's perception of the organization. It is the controlling and managing of these many functions that make an organization ideally consumer-centric. Placing the customer at the center of the business paradigm requires, first and foremost, that the customer be treated as an individual. Too many organizations formulate their grand strategies in back rooms with little concern for the interests of customers. Planning for customer centricity means planning for the customer's specific needs and desires. Best Buy is an excellent example of an organization that has witnessed phenomenal growth and success through an approach that letting the customer decide the company's direction. Best Buy began as a small record store and today it is a major retailer selling virtually every product that has anything to do with consumer electronics. Key to the chain profitability was its decision.

Stores must become customer-segmented and be built around the unique interests of customers in each area. Rather than have a cookie-cutter approach to design and stocking that fit corporate needs for efficiency and control, stores must reflect customer needs. More autonomy would be given to store managers and technology must be employed to keep on top of customer buying patterns. Processes that were not customer-driven must be driven out: readjusted, or eliminated. (Bill, 2006).

The new concept means that Best Buy's management and employees actively listen to their clientele. In each location, the public would be permitted to shape the look, feel, and appeal of the retail store. If in one area customers were not buying a given product it would not be stocked. If customers asked for a certain kind of music, managers would make sure to provide that kind of music. Consumer tastes and preferences were avidly followed permitting local managers to come up with a store that was uniquely tailored to those who shopped in it. It was if consumers were being asked to create their own ideal electronics, music and video retailer. In a sense, one could say that Best Buy looked to one of its products for answers. In the name of consumer- centrism, they took the concept behind video games like that SimCity Series, and similar offering such as those that allows the user to design an amusement park, zoo, prison, etc. and applied it to the real-life situation of Best Buy's retail business.

This newer approach is about everything that happens after the orders are placed. The focus is on order creation as customer specifications become more important and products configuration, flexible pricing models, and remote order management take over. In essence, the customer is taking over as chief architect of a manufacture's future product development.

The Acer Corporation is just one example of a company that takes this concept a step further, building the idea of quick response to customer needs into its corporate organizational structure. The computer manufacturer instituted what is called a "fast food" strategy of manufacturing and sales. As at popular food outlets such as McDonald's or Burger King, Acer's operations were split between a slow cycle and a fast cycle according to responsiveness needs. Powers supplies and disk drivers–items that do not change frequently-could be assembled in Asia without regard to pressing time constraints, while microprocessors and RAM–components that are constantly changing in accord with new technologies–could be shipped to regional distribution centers at the last possible moment. Acer's "Fast Food" strategy permits the customer to dictate what she or he wants and needs most. Computer-savvy individuals and small business owners need to frequently change microprocessors and RAM in order to keep up to date. They may make these changes at any time, without necessarily changing the larger, bulkier, and more permanent hardware associated with their machines. Acer categorizes its all of its manufacturing facilities as SBU's, slow business units, or RBU's, Regional Business Units. This Formal division within the organization has benefited Acer enormously by allowing the company to become markedly more innovative in product design. Once more, the customer centric approach, specifically as it applied to responsiveness to the "unique customer" has helped to improve profitability and competitiveness.

In today's business world, customer centric organizations may take advantage of applications that are specially designed to handle the overall problems of customer relations. Customer Relationship Management or CRM can be defined as an ongoing process that involves the development and leveraging of market intelligence for purpose of building and maintaining a profit maximizing portfolio of customer relationships (Zablah et al., 2004). Broadly speaking, CRM is intended to help providers develop maximally profitable customer base by enabling them to acquire and centrally store information (i.e., intelligence) about current and prospective customers which they can utilize to: (1) prioritize customer relationships according to their long term value to the firm and (2) craft "high quality" interactions that take into consideration each customer's unique set of needs and preferences (Zablah et al., 2004). The underlying assumption is that CRM leads to desirable relationship outcomes (and thus improved organizational performance) because customers tend to naturally "gravitate" towards those providers that are able to consistently deliver "superior" interactions-vis-à-vis competitors – over time.

Relationship Management concept is developed by D. Nelson (2003): a business strategy that maximizes profitability, revenue and customer satisfaction by organizing around customer segments, fostering behaviour that satisfies customers and implementing customer-centric processes. To achieve the long-term value of CRM, enterprises must understand that it is a strategy involving the whole business. Since the emergence of CRM technologies, the market for CRM-related products and services has grown substantially. In fact, early projections suggest that by the end of 2007, yearly global expenditures on CRM technology are likely to exceed $ 17 billion (Aberdeen Group, 2003). As customer relation is such a broad area, embracing customers' need and questions, as well as the sales and support aspects of a business as they relate directly to the customer, it is important that the process of understanding and managing it be made as simple and straight forward as possible. CRM is all about treating different customers differently. CRM should not be seen as a technology, it is a capability for organization. With a CRM platform, organizations will be able to make more effective and faster business decisions. CRM capability is a critical ingredient for customer centricity. To make the CRM business strategy successful, organizations need to change the organization structure based on culture segments and change the company culture to adopt the new CRM strategy.

First among these tasks is market automation. Marketing automation software focuses on promotion and advertising. Advertising campaigns conducted in connection with e-commerce can range from the traditional i.e., newspaper and magazine advertisements, television and radio commercials, and telemarketing operations to those forms of promotion specific to the online environment, such as web pop-ups, banners, e-mail solicitations and so forth. Market automation software can handle the distribution of these announcements as well as track their effectiveness by monitoring sales that result from advertising campaigns or by recording the reactions of those targeted by these advertising campaigns.

The ability to control all aspects of marketing is critical to achieving success in today's global markets. Companies are becoming increasingly short-term oriented. Marketing executives are often judged on the basis of the short-term sales evolution of the products and brands for which they are responsible. However, the impact of many communications tools, such as advertising, sponsorship and marketing public relations become apparent in the long run. Their impact is often cognitive (e.g., increased brand awareness) or attitudinal (e.g., a better brand image). Market automation software makes it easier for businesses to track current developments and to use this information to predict future trends. The global reach of many of today's business produces an unprecedented volume of data. The better a business is able to organize and understand the data flows, the better will it be able to operate in this new and highly competitive environment.

Next on the list of customer relationship management applications is sales automation software. The idea behind sales automation software is to create a virtual salesperson who can perform the necessary functions of tracking prospects and cataloguing contact information. This software must closely match the needs of the company. In order to determine if a sales automation application will provide an acceptable return on investment it is advisable to compare the make-up of a list of prospects to the record of sales obtained by those prospects. After the project has been implemented, the company must use the numeric information's quantitative results to test the assumptions and see how the project is contributing to revenue or cost goal. Regular measurement—as soon as three months into a project—would show a project team if the system had helped them to gather more qualified leads.

Internet software is able to reproduce the capabilities of current sales paradigms. The idea is to expand the reach of the salesperson. Customer centrism is all about expanding business by being able best to meet customers' needs. By applying sales techniques on a global electronic scale the company can reach out to potential customers in regions to which it previously did not have access.

The third and last category of CRM software consists of support/service automation software. This branch of customer relations is especially important as a business' skill at problem solving can determine whether a customer becomes a repeat customer. Support services would include almost any form of troubleshooting. Merchandise might be delayed or directed to an incorrect address. Severe weather, earthquakes, and other natural disasters might create emergency needs in connection with the movement of goods and services. Support/service software must address all contingencies. Essential too, is the fact that it must be easily accessible to both one's support staff and one's customer base. Related user interface design should also be given especial attention. Research in information systems, especially research on the user interface, strongly suggests that the nature of interface design is an important factor affecting the success of failure of commercial websites. The user intentions, context, knowledge, skills, and experience are the essential things that every designer needs to know.

5

Strategic Alignment

Organizations need executable strategy to achieve business goals in today's competitive global landscape. Resources are getting scarce, and operational efficiency and excellence are key critical assets for organization. The third stage in the authentic customer centricity journey is therefore primarily concerned with strategic alignment (see Figure 5.1). I this Chapter I will discuss how strategic alignment should be designed to accelerate transformation towards customer centricity.

Alignment is the adjustment of an object in relation to other objects so that the arrangement can lead to the optimizing of the position or the relationship between the objects. Strategic alignment is the process of aligning an organization's structure and resources with its strategy and business environment (Rampersad, 2003). It is a business redesign process, in which you align your strategic goals (= what do we want to achieve?), business processes (= how do we want to achieve it?), and company culture with your key business purpose (= why are we here?) and core values (= which are the values and behaviors in line with our purpose?). It is also about bringing the actions of an organization's business divisions and staff mem-

Authentic Customer Centricity, pages 65–73
Copyright © 2015 by Information Age Publishing
All rights of reproduction in any form reserved.

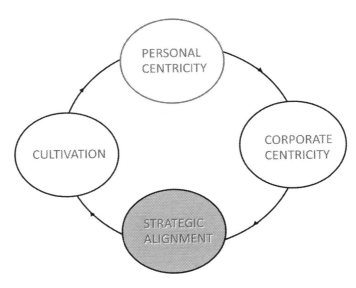

Figure 5.1 Third Stage in the Authentic Customer Centricity Model.

bers in line with the organization's planned objectives, in order to assure that its divisions and employees are jointly working toward the company's stated goals. Good strategic alignment has a strong effect on organizational performance and is essential for becoming a sustainable customer centric company. People perform better when they fully understand and accept the purpose and goals of their organization, and they develop a better sense of ownership when they understand what difference they make in achieving those goals (Rampersad, 2009). It enables higher performance by optimizing the contributions of people, processes, and inputs to the realization of measurable objectives. With strategic alignment, it is possible to improve customer satisfaction more effectively and gain a competitive advantage. Strategic alignment makes no sense without deeply involving your customers (Advance Business Consulting, 2014).

In line with your key business purpose, your core values and your strategic goals, the right business model needs to be chosen. A business model describes how your organization creates and delivers value. Following Geoffrey A. Moore's theory of innovation vectors, any enterprise needs to make fundamental decisions in the choice of the business model in order to support their key business purpose, core values, brand promise, and strategic goals.

Following Moore's theory, we distinguish four different business models (Advance Business Consulting, 2014):

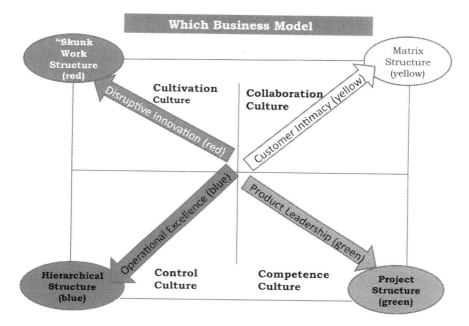

Figure 5.2 Geoffrey A. Moore's Theory of Innovation Vectors (Advance Business Consulting, 2014).

Model 1: The "Disruptive Innovation" Business Model ("Red")

A "disruptive innovation" oriented strategy initiates a growth market by creating a new category through one of these two mechanisms:

- Discontinuous technology: creates new standards incompatible with currently prevailing standards, forcing those who adopt it to displace their existing systems, e.g., Apple;
- Value-chain discontinuity: destabilizes the value chain in an existing market by challenging existing business models, e.g. Southwest Airlines.

The preferred organizational structure for the red strategy is a 'skunk work' structure, creating innovations, improvements and plans in spontaneous and often temporary entities with subjectively defined (or even undefined) metrics. The best culture for this strategy is a 'cultivation culture', where self-actualization, individual accountability and empowerment are key contributors. Examples of "red" companies are Google (however slowly losing its color and turning "green"), Apple, Southwest Airlines (with a touch of "yellow"), and Virgin.

Model 2: The "Customer Intimacy" Business Model ("Yellow")

The "customer intimacy" oriented strategy focuses on making flexible and differentiated value propositions by aligning them more precisely with target customers' needs and values. This strategy requires close customer proximity, and relies heavily on accurate market- and customer intelligence. Customer intimacy does not necessarily call for increasing customer satisfaction. It requires taking responsibility for customer results. It does not impose arm's length goodwill. It requires down-in-the-trenches solidarity, the exchange of useful information, and a collaborative pursuit of results. The preferred organizational structure for this strategy is a 'matrix structure', where different disciplines are closely collaborating in a matrix model, providing the best possible individually tailored customer offerings. The best culture for this strategy is a culture of 'collaboration', rooted in the need for affiliation, and characterized by team-level accountability to subjectively determined metrics.

A clear example of a "yellow" company is Dell Computers. Dell was the first personal computer company to organize and build itself around the idea of direct customer feedback.

> Our attitude was diametrically opposed to the engineering-driven thinking of "Let's invent something and then go push it onto customers who might be willing to buy it." Instead, I founded the company with the intention of creating products and services based on a keen sense of the customer's input and the customer's needs. I spend about 40% of my time with customers

says Michael Dell. Dell has a touch of "red" as well, since their strategy of selling direct through the Internet is a clear example in their industry of disruptive *'value chain discontinuity'*.

Another example of a "yellow" company is within the otherwise very *green* Bayer group: Nunhems Vegetable Seeds. Nunhems Vegetable Seeds is a relatively small but extremely successful international plant genetics company, specialized in breeding vegetable seed varieties. Nunhems successfully competes with giants like Syngenta and Monsanto, and for almost ten years in row, Nunhems is the benchmark in the industry for growth and profitability. Like Dell, Nunhems also has a touch of "red"; Nunhems' unique and daring strategy of selling directly to vegetable growers instead of through dealers is an example of *'value chain discontinuity'*.

Model 3: The "Product Leadership" Business Model ("Green")

The "product leadership" oriented strategy focuses on differentiating market offerings by creating more desirable features, better performance, or lower market price. It mainly creates a growth market position by using research and development to improve features, performance, or market price in an established product category. The preferred organizational structure for this business model is a 'project structure'. In this structure, officially appointed project teams and departments work along objectively defined metrics.

The best culture for this business model is a 'competence culture'. This culture is rooted in the need for achievement and characterized by individual-level accountability to objectively defined metrics. Examples of "green" companies are Bayer, Hewlett Packard, Microsoft, Philips, and Syngenta.

Model 4: The "Operational Excellence" Business Model ("Blue")

The "operational excellence" oriented strategy focuses on optimizing processes and systems to differentiate offerings by lower cost, higher quality, or faster time to market. The preferred organizational structure for this business model is the hierarchical structure, in which processes and systems are fixed in protocols, the following of which is mandatory. The best culture for this business model is a 'control culture'. The control culture is rooted in the need for order and security and characterized by team-level accountability to objectively defined metrics. Examples of "blue" companies are General Motors, Compaq (before the takeover by HP), Eastman Kodak, General Electric, and TNT.

Figure 5.3 shows a diagram with some of the typical behaviors in the different business models.

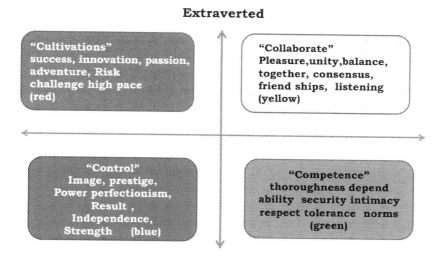

Figure 5.3 Some of the Typical Behaviors in the Different Business Models (Advance Business Consulting, 2014).

Lack of strategic alignment is one of the major causes for organizations to fail. Often this is caused by growth and diversification, often by shareholder centered rather than customer centered behavior, often because the self-centered rather than customer centered objectives of top management. As a result of this the strategic goals, business processes and organizational culture become misaligned, employees lose their focus, and customers lose their faith (Rampersad, 2003). In order to assure long-term success, organizations need to align their strategy, their organizational structure, and their organizational culture into one color. Some examples of poorly aligned organizations are:

- TNT—pretends to be yellow, organized itself green, has a blue business culture;
- Eastman Kodak—presents itself yellow, but has a blue organizational model, and a blue business culture;
- General Motors—has tried yellow initiatives like Saturn, but is slowed down by a very blue HQ.

STATEGIC ALIGNMENT BUSINESS CASES

The impact of strategic (mis)alignment is demonstrated by the striking difference in performance between some of the largest corporations in the world, see next section. The market in which they compete is the same, their chances are the same, and still some thrive and others don't. The description of these business cases is derived from Advance Business Consulting (2014).

The Rise of Southwest Airlines

Southwest Airlines is probably one of the most striking examples of a company that (a) defined a very clear and simple key business purpose, (b) chose the right business model to support the business purpose, and (c) consistently demonstrates the core values and behaviors derived from that key business purpose. The brand promise of Southwest Airlines is *'Dedication to the highest quality of Customer Service delivered with a sense of warmth, friendliness, individual pride, and Company Spirit'*. Every single employee of the company is aligned with this brand promise, and in spite of the current economic turmoil in the airline industry Southwest's performance in 2008 was among the best in the industry. Staff morale is exceptionally high.

The Demise of Northwest Airlines

Northwest Airlines is the striking opposite, and an example of a poorly aligned organization with low staff morale, occupied in a constant struggle against bankruptcy. Northwest's brand promise is *'Safety. Reliability. Comfort. Fairness. Courtesy. Honesty'*, followed by a page long sum up of promises of which very few are made true to customers. Employees don't seem to be involved in the brand promise, and everyone who has traveled with Northwest can account for the personal indifference and the lack of fairness and courtesy many of the staff demonstrate.

The Rise of Toyota

Toyota is another benchmark example of a company with excellent strategic alignment. In spite of its size and complexity Toyota has managed to keep its strategy, organization and people perfectly aligned with its main purpose: *pursuit of harmonious growth* and *enhancement of profitability*. Toyota is driven by this corporate purpose, and the purpose is clearly understood and internalized by its senior management and employees. At Toyota employees are continuously trained in 'The Toyota Way', and a continuous and overall attention for product quality and cost awareness becomes an almost religious way of life for everyone in the organization.

The Demise of General Motors

What does strategic alignment have to do with the demise of the once largest automobile manufacturer in the world? *Everything!* When the purpose and brand values of your company aren›t clear, there will never be a clear strategy. Without a clear purpose and strategy people do not focus, and are not be able to identify with their brand and what it stands for. GM›s internal organization has been stifled by bureaucracy for decades, its production has been hampered by strikes, and its marketing has since long lost track of the developments in the outside world where car buyers have continuously been disappointed by the failing reliability and lack of fuel efficiency of the GM cars they bought.

Alignment has to happen on all organizational levels, as shown in Figure 5.4 (Rampersad, 2003). The related strategic plan must be created against the backdrop of the organization's values, which lay the foundation for the accepted behaviors in the organization.

The competencies required to ensure strategic alignment are an important inclusion into the strategy skill set that leaders in organizations need. The work by Sergay Group (2014) indicates they need to be able to:

- take a big picture perspective on problems, decisions, situations and events
- identify key stakeholders within the organization and within the marketplace or industry with whom your team needs to interact
- ascertain political agendas and adjust your decisions and actions accordingly
- integrate and assimilate information

Figure 5.4 Alignment on All Organizational Levels (The Sergay Group, 2014).

- understand the interrelationships between issues
- recognize causal relationships
- be aware of the multiple effects of any actions decided upon
- view information from different perspectives and points of view, to interpret implications, and to make appropriate recommendations
- identify common elements or trends in situations and actions
- ensure strategic alignment between the macro-environment and the organization
- ensure alignment between different areas in the organization
- appreciate the pressures that each functional group experiences in the organization and work to mitigate them
- make decisions taking into account all the relevant variables
- make decisions that are aligned to the organization's needs
- breakdown strategy into a practical performance plan to achieve it

All that gets done in an organization needs to be aligned to each other, as well as the strategy, in order to help achieve the strategic goals. Strategic pillars for customer centricity means finding the right organizational model, instituting right culture, right value chain and right investment in right human capital. Aligning these strategic pillars is a must to attain customer centricity.

6

Cultivation

Cultivating all the key ingredients employee satisfaction, right organizational model, right strategic pillars is the final phase towards effective customer centricity. The fourth stage in the authentic customer centricity journey focuses on this issue (see Figure 6.1). This stage targets to achieve a stable basis for delivering superior customer experience in your organization's competitive landscape.

6.1 Customer Experience

J. Kirkby et al. (2003) define customer experience as the delivery of the company's brand promise to its customers. This experience occurs at every touch point such as contact centers, sales people, advertising, events and others. The customer experience is filtered through customers' expectation of the company which is determined by the customer's value proposition and feedback from other customers, see Figure 6.2.

The classic transaction marketing has transformed into relationship marketing. In order to motivate the customers to turn to the company

Authentic Customer Centricity, pages 75–83
Copyright © 2015 by Information Age Publishing
All rights of reproduction in any form reserved.

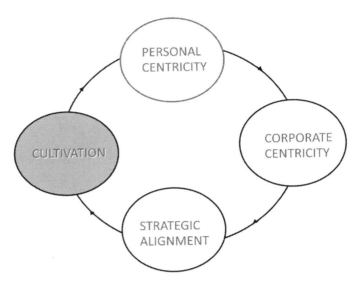

Figure 6.1 Fourth Stage in the Authentic Customer Centricity Model.

Figure 6.2 Customer Experience Management (J. Kirkby and J. Wecksell, 2003).

goods and services as often as possible and to purchase more each time, the company and the employees must ensure that each customer's experience with this company is very positive and the customer from an occasional purchaser turns into a loyal golden customer. Companies must improve and develop cumulative customer satisfaction rather than one transaction-specific customer satisfaction. Any company will have value to the customer only if it is able to firstly satisfy or/and exceed customer's expectations. Secondly, as there are different providers of similar products, the customer will also choose by the quality of the service offered and the level their basic needs are satisfied, such as speed of delivery and responsiveness as well as the support of the staff dealing with the customer. Thirdly, the two mentioned above must differentiate the firm from competitors by means of flexible pricing, customized approach to the customers, adaptation of the products and services to exceed customer expectations, and generally positive attitude to the cooperation. These three components will affect the total customer experience/satisfaction with the company. Molineus (2002) emphasizes that customer's decision on which company to deal with depends on three milestones: how, when and at what cost to the customer. More importantly, customers that have already existing relationship with the company, expect to receive quality services all the time they deal with the company, which stresses necessity to train staff to constantly offer best quality services and products. It is vital to match and/or exceed customers' expectations, as due to human psychology, they tend to compare anything to the best they obtained once in the market.

Great customer experience that leads to customer satisfaction is characterized by the following attributes namely, source of competitive advantage, differential by focusing on stimulating emotions, enabled through inspirational leadership and people who are happy and fulfilled, designed outside in rather than inside out, revenue generating and reduce costs. The purpose of a customer experience is to create constructive interactions that make customers come back and enjoy dealing with the company's products and services.

The discussed Customer Relationship Management (CRM) concept has been developed as a tool for managing customer experience by allowing the analysis of historic purchase patterns of the customers within the company and be able to adopt company productions and services.

The quality of customers experience is measured by customer retention rate and customer satisfaction rate, after which the customers can be grouped according by their loyalty to the company. Lindgreen (2004) in his study suggest development of such customer loyalty matrix for this purpose. Changes of the quantity of customers within each segment can reveal effectiveness of the transformation of the company into customer-centric organization. Also, changes in customer satisfaction can reveal effectiveness of implementation of employee motivation systems. For big companies which have many sales account managers it is also necessary to monitor changes in customer loyalty and performance in order to be able to define areas of improvement. J. Kirkby (2003) noted that resolving complaints and improving customer experience at companies' touch points such as contact centers can help to reduce customer defection by 2 percent to 3 percent per year. They continue explaining the stages of customer experience as shown in Figure 6.3. It shows the emotional values customers put on their experiences from feeling of loathing to Zen. The figure provides a way to feel and quantify emotions from a customer experience perspective, and it shows the emotional values customers put on their experiences.

Not every customer will have a Zen experience. The aim is to move customers up the scale based on their potential. Some may never get past "run of the mill"; however, it must be known that a company can deliver satisfaction without gaining loyalty, but not loyalty without satisfaction. Ultimately, the customer experience is a business issue. A poor customer experience can put customers' relationship and stakeholder value at risk and promote value defections and lower shareholder value.

Improving customer satisfaction is just as prevalent as improving employee satisfaction. Many different studies focused on the abilities of new

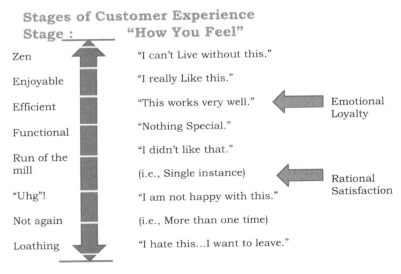

Figure 6.3 Stages of Customer Experience (J. Kirkby, 2003).

technologies to drastically improve customer service. Businesses are now able to personalize and improve interactions with every customer, and across every point-of-contact, thanks to new technologies for information capture and analysis. Customers receive precisely the information they need, when they need it and how they need it, while businesses are able to manage relationships more effectively, efficiently and profitably through all avenues of interaction. Many studies suggest the need for organizations to focus on their level of service delivery to the customer.

Most companies lose 45% to 50% of their customers every five years, winning new customers can be up to 20 times more expensive than retaining existing customers (Full 2006). The higher the level of satisfaction that customers experience, the greater the trust and confidence they show. As this trust and confidence grows, they will be less likely to move their business for a few percentage points (Castiglione 2006). When it comes to measuring their customers' satisfaction, too many companies have settled into a comfortable rut of changing their approaches to get the results they want (Columbusn 2005). Competitors that are prospering in the new global economy recognize that measuring customer satisfaction is key. Only by doing so can they hold on to the customers they have and understand how to better attract new customers.

The literature on the improvement of customer satisfaction considered the importance of measuring what matters to customers. This information is critical to understanding exactly what you need to fix. For example, if the customers are particularly dissatisfied with some aspect of the organization's service, but it is discovered that the thing they are unhappy with is not important to them, then the organization can focus on what is important for increasing customer satisfaction. An effective way to measure and gauge customer expectations and satisfaction is through the use of Customer Relationship Management tools. Maintaining control of customer relationships is possible only through consistent implementation of classic, well-proven customer bonding techniques, such as individualized customer care and communications, rewards for customer value and loyalty, special consideration for high-value customers and customized products and services (Ferruzza 1999). Implementing customer relationship management strategies is the most effective way to accomplish this. Greenberg (2006) stated that employee and customer satisfaction are considered to be one of the priorities for organizations committed to customer centricity and continuous improvement, both internally and externally.

6.2 Elements of Delivering Superior Customer Experience

This section focuses on several specific areas of customer service that should be considered by any organization attempting to raise customer service standards and become a customer centric organization. It almost goes without saying that good customer service is essential to sustaining any business. No matter how wonderful a job you do of attracting new customers, you won't be profitable for long unless you have a solid customer retention strategy in place that includes delivering great customer service. Customers are not concerned with a policy statement or the promise of exceptional service. They remember how they have been treated by the organization's employees and what actions were taken to satisfy their needs (Clark, 2006). As to this point, there are several specific considerations for those employees of the organization that come into contact with customers. Most consumers have a desire to receive good customer service. Quite often, they desire the little things like common courtesies, efficient service, and appropriate attention (Wheelihan, 2002).

Here are some essential elements of providing great customer service that contribute to become customer centric:

Engaging customers—It is tough to exaggerate the importance of customer engagement. Fully engaged customers deliver a 23% premium over average customers in share of wallet, profitability, revenue, and relationship growth, according to Gallup Research, while actively disengaged customers represent a 13% discount on the same measures. Furthermore, workgroups that are in the top 25% based on their levels of customer engagement outperform the rest on measures of profit, sales, and growth by a factor of two to one (Rieger, 2006). Engaging the customer is one of the first steps to providing customer service that will make a lasting impression on the customer.

Be accessible—Customers expect, justifiably so, that they will have access to employees for questions and concerns, whether on the phone or in person. This element of customer service should be addressed in an organizations customer service strategy. An effective strategy will set the stage and define minimum levels of accessibility for customer access. The expectations of accessibility should be defined and taught to all employees of the organization. Employees should never be too busy to be accessible to customers. An organization should consider investments in the infrastructure that are necessary to provide accessible customer service. This may mean the addition of more people, redesigning physical facilities, or changing the hours of operation for the organization. Whatever the initiative, the goal should be to allow for the maximum accessibility possible for the customer.

Be reliable—Reliability means keeping the promise you made to the customer and doing what you say you will do for the customer. It is important to keep in mind that promises are not only made directly and verbally, but through a myriad of delivery paths in various forms. Organizations make direct promises to customers through advertising and marketing materials, in company correspondence and contracts, and in service guarantees and policies published for everyone to see. In addition, customers will hold the company to indirect commitments – promises that customers believe are implied in the way the company talks about itself, its products, and its services (Zemke, 2003). Not keeping promises is one of the quickest ways to create disgruntled, former customers.

Display the right attitude—Persons' attitude color the way they react to customers because it has a direct effect on what they hear and how they respond. There are people who can find opportunity in any adversity. Outgoing and optimistic, they strive to make customer engagements fun. They inspire a contagious enthusiasm and make others around them better (Freiberg, 2005). Customers sense this and react better to these types of people. Displaying the right attitude is important for everyone in the organization in pursuing an atmosphere that promotes great customer service. Manners count when dealing with customers. Be polite and exhibit an empathetic attitude toward customers.

Accept responsibility—Everyone makes mistakes. The key to rectifying a mistake is to be honest with the customer and to accept responsibility. The absolute best way to establish a sterling reputation as an organization is to be prepared to take responsibility for whatever decision you make. It is a matter of integrity, and it will earn you the respect of both the employees and customers of the organization (Scott, 2001, Rampersad, 2014). Accepting responsibility also means being a team player and providing service to the customer on behalf of the entire organization. There can be no "it's not my job." When a mistake has been made, admit it and set things straight. When customers have a complaint—listen, truly listen. Then, apologize and take corrective action. In many instances, the very act of listening (without interrupting) can be enough to diffuse the situation and make the person feel worthy as a customer (Clark, 2006).

Be responsive—Timeliness has always been an important part of delivering great customer service, but in today's hurried society, it has become even more important. From fast food restaurants to one-hour photo finishing, customers are demanding faster service than ever before. Companies that cater to time conscious customers are everywhere you look. Their success affects your customers' expectations of your willingness and ability to do the same. When customers see other organizations delivering faster and more efficient service, they will demand it of your organization as well (Zemke, 2003). If an organization is unable to be as responsive as their competitors, they run the risk of delivering undesirable customer service, or at worst, losing customers to the competition.

Be empathetic—Being empathetic toward customers shows them that you care about their situation. Take time to listen to their concerns, and take actions that show you care. We are used to thinking of compassion as an emotional state, based on our concern for one another. But it is also grounded in a level of awareness. People see more of the systems within which they operate, and as they understand more clearly the pressures influencing one another, they naturally develop more compassion and empathy (Senge, 1990). To be truly empathetic with a customer an employee should put himself/herself in the position of the customer. Recognizing the customer's emotional state helps an organization figure out the best way to effectively provide them the service that they are looking for.

Be there for the customer—In many ways, "being there" is the culmination of all of the previous elements mentioned. However, it is also a state of mind. It means that you are present at that time, at that moment, for the customer and his or her needs take precedents over any other function. How much do you actually get done when you are in one place thinking about a different place? Why not commit to being in one place at one time? When you are present, not dwelling on what happened in the past or worried about what may happen in the future, you are fully attuned to opportunities that develop and to the needs of the people you encounter. You gain a healthier perspective and the capacity for greater focus and creativity (Lundin et al., 2002). Customers will easily recognize when they are the sole focus of an employee.

Monitor achievement—Measurement is both the first and last step in producing superior service. There is little sense in creating extensive measurement systems until all the other elements of service are in place, or until there is something to measure. But drafting an effective strategy, the first step toward better service, is difficult without some measure of current service performance. Measuring service performance or quality is quite different from measuring product quality because service is an experience. The best measurement systems focus on the three aspects of service: process, product, and customer satisfaction (Klein, 1999). Measuring elements of the service profit chain provides an overall indication of how an organization is doing, particularly on dimensions important to the business such as customer service. It is important that the methods of measurement be understood and consistent from period to period. Organizations that have constructed elaborate measurements and methods often find that the cost of maintaining them and difficulty understanding them defeat their usefulness and guarantee that they will fall into disuse. Such approaches often lead to the kind of tinkering that changes measures from one period to the next, making it impossible to track progress (Heskett, Sasser and Schlesinger, 1997). Great service is much like a gift; it makes us want to continue to do business with an organization on a repetitive basis into the future. With so much competition in the marketplace, customer loyalty is at a premium. The best way to ensure customer loyalty is by consistently delivering great customer service. You achieve customer loyalty by doing the little things that make customers want to deal with the organization again and again, and recommend the organization to others.

Satisfying customers can be a tricky endeavor when organizations are faced with multiple complaints, demands, personalities, and angry customers. When these situations arise, the best course of action is to honestly and expeditiously address them. Employees should listen to the customer's concern, empathize with their situation, and take actions to rectify the situation (Selland, 2006). One of the more important factors mentioned in this section is to be "present" for the customer. Above all else, if customers really feel that you are solely attending to their needs, they will experience a feeling of importance that will translate into a positive customer service experience for them.

With the hyper-expansion of the "virtual" economy more and more customer transactions are taking place in a virtual environment. These customers too expect great customer service. Just as in face-to-face transactions, customers expect virtual transactions to contain the essential elements of customer service. A recent study done on Internet customer service found that satisfaction with various elements of Internet customer service is not at the levels many would expect. According to the respondents, only 43 percent were satisfied with e-mail as a customer service vehicle. Thirty-four percent were satisfied with Web sites in general as a mode of customer service (Rohrbacher, 2001). These numbers indicate the need for organizations that do business in an online environment to better adhere to desired customer service principles.

Cultivating a superior customer experience is absolute necessity for sustainability of organizations. Today word of mouth is the winning marketing formula. Internet has been disintermediated the value chains between end users and suppliers, so whoever wins the customer experience will win the market share game in the most sustainable and profitable way.

7

A Real Life Example

Business Case

To illustrate the authentic customer centricity model, I successfully applied the authentic customer centricity framework into a call center business. The implementation entails 5 phases as illustrated in Figure 7.1.

In the first phase, I recommend that the project is authorized and aligned with corporate objectives and key personnel are assembled. This key personnel team should comprise a project champion, a Call Centre Transformation Team (CCTT), a lead director and a lead consultant. This team needs to review and validate the recommendations regarding the implementation of the project, the expected benefits and the KPI's by which it will be managed. The CCTT needs to present its recommendations to the Management Committee of the company chaired by the CEO and request approval to proceed with the main implementation phases. The second phase entails 'Prepare and Energize Staff'. In this phase, there are two parallel work streams: One to prepare the new tools and processes, the second to send a signal to all staff that a challenging change to a new customer-centric way of thinking and behaving is being introduced. The

Authentic Customer Centricity, pages 85–92
Copyright © 2015 by Information Age Publishing
All rights of reproduction in any form reserved.

Figure 7.1 Implementation Model of the Proposed Authentic Customer Centricity Model.

third phase entails 'Activate & Enthuse Staff'. This is a process of culture change to be focused on customer centricity and satisfaction. The fourth phase is 'Finalize and Implement' the new call center operational model. This is the implementation of the background work that has been carried out by the support functions and modified by agent feedback and other learning derived during phases 2 and 3. The final phase entails 'Review and Improve'—a constant process of monitoring, feedback, learning, adaptation and improvement. These five phases and their inter-relationship are shown in Figure 7.1. I will discuss each phase in detail in the next sections.

Phase 1

The call center GM must set up the CCTT as described, reporting directly to himself and be assembled as follows in order to achieve the recommendations set out in this section:

- ▪ CCTT Executive Director (ED): This is an executive who will be the full-time leader of the program, carrying operational responsibility for a successful implementation.

- Lead Consultancy: A program of this scope and duration will require substantial dedicated effort and expertise. A suitable consultancy will bring in knowledge and awareness of international best practice and benchmarks, as well as industry skills to complement the skills of the company. It will also relieve some of the load on company management.
- The ED will be further supported by the Directors of the following functions, each of whom will appoint a suitably skilled leader to be a dedicated full-time member of the implementation team:
  - The *Director of Customer Experience*, whose function will be to input the company's current and on-going measures of customer satisfaction, the key messages the company wishes to deliver and new products and services as they are being brought to market.
  - The *HR Director*, whose function will be to organize the training program, any necessary recruitment, to advice on the KPI's and agent incentive programs and their alignment with company practice and objectives. This will cover training in behavior, processes and use of the various support systems. The scale of training required will require HR to develop an initial set of experts, and then a train-the-trainer program to match the target deployment.
  - The *Director of Internal Communications*, who will be responsible for delivering the appropriate messages about the program not only to the Call Centre staff, but to the company as a whole. He will also be responsible for providing a mechanism to capture, analyze and act on feedback from the call center agents and their supervisors.
  - The *IT Director*, whose function will be to provide access to the two key sets of tools required by the agents: The operational diagnostic tools which enable an agent to understand any technical issue affecting the customer and the customer relationship management (CRM) tools that give the agent all the information he needs about the customer and his or her history with the company.
- CCTT should then recruit the lead consultancy. This should be done in the following stages:
  - Define the specification for the lead consultancy as a company with a proven international track record in culture change in service industry preferably telecom sector and specifically in call centers.

- Issue a request for information (RFI) to companies considered to be suitably qualified.
- Issue a request for proposal (RFP) to a shortlist of selected companies from submissions received.
- Bring the selected company into the CCTT activities.

▪ CCTT and Consultant should then agree on an overall implementation plan for each of the five phases, as recommended. This will include a number of review points at which progress will be formally reviewed, with the remaining timetable adapted as necessary.

▪ CCTT, supported by the Consultant, will then present the program to the company's Management Committee members and President, describing the five stages of implementation, the program plan, the expected benefits and the KPI's by which achievement of these will measured.

▪ The approval by the Management Committee should be marked by a personal message from the President and should be the moment to ignite the program in the minds of the employees.

▪ CCTT should then hold a launch briefing to call center agents and supervisors, explaining the program objectives and scope, the roles of the project team, and the roles that the supervisors and agents will play during the implementation.

▪ This should be followed by the set-up of the various internal communications vehicles to be used, both for outbound messaging to staff and for collecting feedback from agents and supervisors.

Phase 2

This stage is about preparing and energizing the staff, both in the Call Centers, and also in the supporting functions that will be developing and implementing the new processes. As mentioned above, the support staff will be engaged in creating and providing the enablers – two-way communications, the diagnostic and CRM tools and processes for their use, the training and the alignment with company customer experience objectives and new products and services. This is about creating a mind-set of customer centricity, customer satisfaction and a winning spirit of "Together we can achieve this!" I propose three recommendations for this phase:

▪ Develop new call scripts that identify lessons learned in this research and identify roles and responsibilities for agents. This must not be interpreted as wrapping the agent in a strait-jacket, but rather as providing a common set of forms of address for greeting, apology if necessary, resolution, proactive offering of other services and final closure. The process of using the diagnostic tools and discussing the findings with the customer or discussing the customer's service requirement cannot be scripted and this is where the skill and knowledge of the agent plays its part. This will contribute in facilitating and improving agent interaction with callers and will create the desired awareness level among agents of their responsibilities and impact.

■ Develop and institutionalize Root Cause Analysis processes for those different scenarios requiring analysis, such as common customer complaints and high repeat callers. This will identify roadblocks, inefficient processes, inconsistent policies and opportunities for automation – the basis for a more lean and effective organization. The result of the removal of such roadblocks, inefficient processes and inconsistent policies will be an improvement in call center efficiency and proactivity. It will also enhance the percentage achieved of first call resolution (FCR) and decrease repeat callers.

■ Enhance team communication within the call center. The objective of this recommendation is to improve the communication within the team and between senior management, agents and supervisors. Performance will be defined by progress against the project plan and progress against the target KPI's as described earlier. As well as the standard management reviews of the above, there will be regular peer group workshops at supervisor and manager level, to identify, for example, individual cases of best practice and how these can be applied, or to identify common problems, which the project team should resolve. The expected impact of this recommendation is to promote team spirit among the agents, improve visibility on performance through regular meetings with them, and promote awareness among agents on the importance of the KPI's, and encourage them to provide feedback as an input to Phase 4.

Phase 3

This phase is to activate and enthuse the call center staff. It takes the attention-grabbing activities in Phase 2 and introduces culture change, specific quality enhancement, and greater focus on customer centricity and satisfaction. There are three specific recommendations to be carried out in this phase as follows:

- Launch an agent culture change program to change the existing cultural norms of the agents and supervisors to be more customer centric and the acceptance of new KPIs being introduced to monitor call center and agent performance. This recommendation will enhance and increase awareness and shift focus to customer centricity with operational efficiency as a key support – a means to an end rather than an end in itself.
- Increase the authority and empowerment of front-line agents to build customer centricity and customer focus at call center. Empowering the agents will enable them to respond faster to customer needs and resolve a defined list of customer service requests without resorting to the back office.
- Introduce live call monitoring to the agent quality assessment process in addition to recorded calls, in order to improve the level of feedback provided to agents. The steps to implement this recommendation involve:
  - Develop the call center's ability to conduct live–call-monitoring.
  - Train staff members in the use of new systems to monitor calls efficiently and properly. In particular, train supervisors to show an agent how the call could have been better handled or to commend an agent on the way he turned around an angry customer and resolved the situation.
  - Design an agent rating process based on the recommended component of agent quality rating KPI's.
  - Train staff members in effectively rating agents.

Phase 4

This phase is about finalizing and implementing the new call center operational model. This is the implementation of the background work that has been carried out by the support functions and modified by agent feedback and other learning derived during Phases 2 and 3. There are five specific recommendations in this phase as follows:

- Develop and deliver a training program for call center agents which focuses on customer satisfaction, use of new tools, skill enhancement and effective utilization of call center resources.

This will certainly contribute to increasing the agent's quality of service, customer satisfaction and morale.

- Provide the agents with the proper tools that will enable them to better analyze customer problems and have access to the right information. These tools have four elements: The diagnostic tools used to investigate a customer's service problem, the CRM system that describes the customer's service set and history, the product and service database and lastly, the processes that guide an agent through the use of all of these. This will improve customer satisfaction by enabling agents to better serve customers and improve FCR by providing agents with tools that help resolve customer problems

- Review the set of KPI's based on the recommendations set out in this book. The training and internal messaging need to explain to both the call center agents and to the company as a whole, the basis upon which these KPI's have been constructed, so that that the link between KPI, individual performance and customer satisfaction is clear to the whole organization.

- Redesign the agent incentive program to align the agent's personal and functional performance with the new customer-centric objectives. This will recognize both his individual responsibilities and his role as a team member.

- Introduction of newly recommended KPIs into the daily reporting process, such as (FCR) and (FRR). A prerequisite for this recommendation is to ensure the presence of necessary systems and processes to measure and report KPIs. The implementation team should create a series of reports from the GM, down to individual agent, and create a publishable version both for all call center staff and all other concerned parties in the company. Clearly care needs to be taken about both individual and company sensitivity. The adoption of this recommendation will provide the tools to monitor and improve performance as well as accountability, ownership and enhance the call center's operational efficiency.

The totality of implementing the four actions in this phase comprises the launch of the program and the new operational process will then be live.

Phase 5

This phase entails Review & Improve. The feedback phase is an essential part of this program, as in any major change initiative. Derning (1986) revealed fourteen key principles for transforming business effectiveness. The fifth of these is the necessity to improve constantly and forever, the system of production and service to improve quality and productivity. It is very important that the company management adopts this approach in driving through its transformation of call centers to being models of customer centricity. The value of this is re-enforced by Derning's championing of the Shewart improvement cycle (sometimes called the Deming improvement cycle) – Plan, Do, Check, Act. I recommend that the project team should not be disbanded immediately after the conclusion of Phase 4, but be kept in place for up to two years beyond that in order to drive the review, learning and adaptation processes. By regularly reviewing agent and customer feedback and call center performance, management will recognize the many areas in which processes, tools, training and attitude can be further changed and enhanced. Massive training effort is required by the organization to instill the courage to break with tradition. The attitude of the agents and call center management is as critical to the success of the transformation program as any process, and it is very important that in the face of operational difficulties, changed attitudes are not allowed to slowly drift back to their previous state. The processes themselves, such as root cause analysis, can never be considered as finished, but always capable of further upgrading and the 'Review & Improve' phase must be institutionalized to facilitate this continuous improvement.

References and Recommended Reading

Advance Business Consulting, 2014 http://www.advancebusinessconsulting. com/advance!/strategic-alignment.aspx

Abredeen Group (2003) 'Worldwide CRM Spending: Forecast and analysis 2002–2006'

Accel Team (2006). *Employee Motivation Theory and Practice.* Available at:, www. accelteam.com/motivation/theory_01.html, (Accessed: August 11, 2006)

Accessed August 10, 2006 from www.adamssixsigma.com/newsletters.htm

Adams. (2006) *Employee Empowerment. Adams six sigma.* Adams associates.

Adebanjo, D. Kehoe. D. (2001), 'An Evolution of Factors Influencing Team-work and Customer Focus', *Managing Service Quality.*

A-H. Maslow (1943) 'A Theory of Human Motivation', *Psychological Review,* Vol. 50

Ahn, J. Y. (2004), *Some aspects on the Web Data Mining for Effecting eCRM from A Statistical Viewpoint,* PhD dissertation, Chonbuk National University, Chonju.

Allen, Gemmy/ (1998). 'Theories of motivation', *Modern management.*

American Productivity and Quality Center (2001) 'The Customer-Centric Contact Center: a New Model', Huston: Texas.

American Productivity and Quality Center Report, (2001), *The Customer Centric Contact Center: A new Model,* U. S. A., Houston, Texas: pp. 50 – 139.

Amerup – Cooper B. And Eduardsson B.(1988).

Anders Gustafsson and Michael D. Johnson, (2000), *Increase Customer Satisfaction, Loyalty, and Profit: An Integrated Measurement and Management System,* San Francisco: Jossey-Bass, p. 20.

Authentic Customer Centricity, pages 93–102

Copyright © 2015 by Information Age Publishing
All rights of reproduction in any form reserved.

Anderson, Eugene W., Cleas Fonell and Roland T. Rust (1997), 'Customer Satisfaction, Productivity and Profitability: Differences Between Goods and Services', *Marketing Science*, Vol. 16, pp 129 – 45.

Andy Neely, ed., (2002) *Business Performance Management: Theory and Practice*, England, Cambridge: Cambridge University Press.

Ascigil, Semra. (2003).Teamwork: *A Tool for enhancing positive work attitudes?*. Dissertation. Western Kentucky University.

Bailey C. (2006) *Finding the Voice of the Customer*. Available at: www.customercentricity.biz (Accessed: 23/1/ 2007).

Berger Paul D. and Nsds T. Nasr (1998), 'Customer Lifetime Value: Marketing Model and Applications', *Journal of Interactive Marketing*, Vol. 12, pp. 17-30

Bill Stopper (2006) 'Best Buy: Customer Centric innovation,' *Humen Resources Planning*, Vol. 29, No.3.

Blackburn R. S. (1982), 'Dimensions of Structure: A Review and Reappraisal', *Academy of Management Review*, Vol. 7, No. 1, pp.56 -66.

Blake R,R and J. S. Mouton.(1968) *Corporate Excellence through Grid Organization development*, Houston: Gulf Publishing Co.

Blanchard, Ken, Carlos, John, and Alan andooph (1996) *Empowerment takes More Than a Minute*, San Fransico: Berret Kochler Publications Inc.

Bonnie P. Stivers, and Teresa Joyce (2000), "Building a Balanced Performance Management System," *SAM Advanced Management Journal* 65.2: 22.

Booz Allen Hamilton (2004), 'A new Operation Model for Telcos, The Customer Centric Organization', *Booz Allen Hamilton Inc. Study*, pp. 1-5.

Booz Allen Hamilton Inc. (2003), *The customer Centric Bank*, July, V. SA, pp. 104.

Boshaff, c. and G Mels (1995). 'A Casual Model to Evaluate the Relationship Among Supervision, Role Stress, Organizational Commitment and Internal Service Quality', *European Journal of Marketing*, 29, 23-42.

Brandi J. Bush (2001), 'People: Attracting, Retaining, and Motivating,' *The Public Manager* 30.2: 31.

Brintnall, Jim (2005). 'What Makes a Good Reward', *Recognition News*, Vol. 2, No. 2.

Brown JD.(1973) 'The Human Nature of Organizations,' *American Management Association*, New York.

Bruce Mckern, ed., (2003) *Managing the Global Network Corporation* (London: Routledge, p.251.

Butcher, Devid R. (2006) *Employee Empowerment Eliminate, US Versus Them*. Industrial Market Trends. Available at: http://news.thomasnet.com/IMT/archives/2006/.iohtm (Accessed: august 10, 2007).

Buzzel, Robert D. and Bradley Gale (1987), *The PIMs principles: Linking Strategy to Performance*. New York: free press.

Cacioppo, Kevin. (2000). 'measuring and managing Customer satisfaction.' *Quality Digest*, September.

Castiglione, Dennnis J. (2006). "Measuring Customer Satisfaction." PROCOM Management Consultants, White Paper.

Catapult systems (2007) *The key to Great Customer Service Catapult Systems.* Available at: www.catapultsystems.com (Accessed: August 3, 2007).

Champy, James. (1995), *Reengineering Management the Market, the Mandate for New Leadership.* New York: Harper Collins Publishers.

Christopher, M., Payne, A., Ballantyne, D. (1991) *Relationship Marketing: Bringing Quality, Customer Service, and Marketing Together.* Oxford: Butterworth-Heinemann.

Clark, Marry. (2006). "Achieving Adaptability through Employee Empowerment." Winning Workplaces, Feature article.

Claudia Imhoff, Lisa Lofts and Jonathan G. Geiger (2001), *Building the Customer Centric Enterprise,* John Wiley & Sons Inc.

Columbusn, Louis. (2005). 'Measuring Customer Satisfaction like you mean it.' *American quality magazine, Article.,* Available at: www.americanquality.com/artman/publish/printer_637.shtml (Accessed: January 8,2007).

Communication in the workplace. (2006). *Workplace Council* White paper, Available at: www.workplacecouncil.com/communication.htm (Accessed on august 7.2007).

Communications and Information Technology Commission (2006), Available at: http://www.citc.gov.sa/citc (Accessed on 20/12/2006)

Craig Cochran (2006), *Becoming a Customer Focused Organization,* Scott M. Paton.

Cristian Mitreann (2006), *Next Generation Customer Centricity,* American Marketing Association. Available at: http://www.marketingpower.com/content

Dahlagaard, J.J., Kristensen, K&Kenji, G.K. (1998) *Fundamentals of Total Quality Management,* London: Champman and Hall.

Dalton D. R., Todor W. D., Spendolini M. J., Fielding G.T. and Porter L. W. (1980), 'Organization Structure and Performance, A Critical Review', *Academy of Management Review,* Vol.5, No.1, pp.49 – 64.

David Rance, (2007), 'Planning to Become Customer Centric', *GCCRM,* Jan.

David V. Day, and Charles E. Lance (2004), '3 Understanding the Development of Leadership Complexity Through Latent Growth Modeling,' in David V. Day, Stephen J. Zaccaro, and Stanley M. Halpin. *Leader Development for Transforming Organizations: Growing Leaders for Tomorrow.* Mahwah, NJ: Lawrence Erlbaum Associates, p. 54.

Day Gorge S. (1999), *The Market Driven Organization,* New York: Free Press.

Denish Shah, Rolan T. Rust, Prarasuraman A., Richars Stalin and Gorge S. Day (2006), 'The Path to Customer Centricity', *Journal of Services Research,* Volume 9, No. 2, Nov 2006, pp. 113 -124.

Denton, Keith (2004). 'Entrepreneurial Spirit-Employee Empowerment. Feature Article'. *Gale group.*

Dimitrades. Zoe. (2001). *Empowerment in total quality: designing an Implementing Effective Employee Decision –Making Strategies.* Dissertation. University of Piraeus.

Dishpandi, Rohit, John W. Fardey and Frederick E. Webster Jr. (1993), 'Corporate Culture, Customer Orientation and Innovativeness', *Journal of Marketing*, 57 (1), p. 23.

Durcker P. (1954), *The Practice of Management*, New York: Harpercollins.

Edvinsson, L., Malone, M.S. (1997) *Intellectual Capital*, New York, NY: Harper-Collins.

Eric J. Arnould, and Linda L. Price (2006) 'Market-Oriented Ethnography Revisited,' *Journal of Advertising Research*, Vol. 46, No.3.

Erven, Bernard L and Robert a. Milligan. (2001). *Making Employee Motivation a Partnership*. Ohio state university and cooperative Extensions, whitepaper.

Eskildsen, J.K. & Dahlagaard, J.J. (2000) 'A Causal Model for Employee Satisfaction', *Total Quality Management*, Vol.11, No. 8, pp.1081-1094.

Farrukh Naeem (2007) 'Why CRM Can Fail', *Gulf Marketing Review*, May, 2007.

Ferruzza, Gene M. (1999). "Enterprise-Wide Customer Relationship management." *DM Review*, May.

Fisher K. (1994) leading Self-Directed Work Teams, McGraw Hill,Mo

Flaherty, Jane (1997) "Jen Tips to Cultivate Communication." *Innovative Leaders*, vol.6 No.12 December 1997.

Fox John (1998). *Employee Empowerment: An Apprenticeship Model.* Dissertation. Barney school of Business, University of Hartford.

Freiberg, Kevin and Jackie Freiberg. (2005).*Guts! Companies That Blow the doors Off Business-As-Usual*. New York: Doubleday.

Full service. (2006). *Customer satisfaction.*B2B International. Available at: www.b2binternational.com (Accessed: january3,2007).

Gallup organization (2006) 'Leveraging Award and Recognition. Programs'. Available at: www.goalkeeperinc.com. (Accessed on august 3, 2007).

Garbarino, E., Johnson, M. S., (1999) 'The Different Roles of Satisfaction, Trust and Commitment in customer relationships', *Journal of marketing*, Vol.63, April, pp. 70-87.

Gartner, W. B. (1988) 'Who is an Entrepreneur? Is The Wrong Question', *American Journal of Small Business*

Gina Plaglicai Mornson, Joseph L. Gagnon and Herb Keleonberges (2005), 'The customer Centric Store: Delivering the Total Experience', *IBM Retailing Issue Letter*, Nov., Volume 17, pp. 1-6.

Greenberg, Penelope Sue and Ralph H. Greenberg. (2006). "Who needs budgets?" *Strategic Finance*, August, 2006, pp.41-42.

Gronnroos, Christian (1994) 'A Service Quality Model and its Marketing Implications', *European Journal of Marketing*, Vol. 18, No. 4. P. 36

Grupta, Sunil, Donald R. Lehmann and Jennifer Ames Stuart (2004), 'Valuing Customers', *Journal of Marketing Research*, Vol. 41, pp.7-8.

Gummesson, E. (2004) 'Return on relationships (ROR): the value of relationship marketing and CRM in business-to-business contexts', *Journal of Business & Industrial Marketing*, Volume 19, No. 2, pp. 136-148.

Hackman, J.K and G.R Oldham. (1980).*Work Redesign*. NY: Addison-Wesley.

Haley, Carolyn (2006) 'Employee Empowerment: Moving Beyond Words Into Action', Available at: www.supporting.com/newsletter/empowerment. htm (Accessed: August 2008).

Hall, Jay. (1980) 'Interpersonal Style and Corporate Climate: Communications Revisited', in J. A. Shortgren (ed.) *Models for Management: The Structure of Competence* Woodlands: Tx., Telemetrics-International, pp.216-236

Hamel, Gray and C. K. Prahlad (1994), *Competing for the Future,* Boston: Harvard Business School Press.

Hammer, Michael and James Champy (1993) *Reengineering the Corporation A Manifesto for Business Rrevolution.* New York: Harper Collins Publishers.

Harshman, Ellen F. And Caril.Harshman (1999) 'Communicating with Employees: Building on an Ethical Foundation.' *Journal of Business Ethics,*19:3-19,

Hart Christopher W. (1999), 'Customers Are Your Business', *Marketing management,* Vol. 8, pp. 6-7.

Hayes Jason. (2003) *Employee Empowerment: Commerce Bank and Cast-Fab Technologies.* Dissertation. Emporia State University School of Business.

Henry F. (1922) *My Life and the Work,* USA: R. H. Value Publishing

Heskett, James L., Sasser, Earl W. and Leonard Schlesinger (1997), *The Service Profit Chain,* New York: The Free Press.

Hildula, Leslie (1996) 'Empowering Employee Empowerment', *The CPA Journal*

Hornburg C., Workman J. J. P. and Krohmer H. (1999), 'Marketing's Influence Within the Firm', *Journal of Marketing,* Vol. 63, No. 2, pp. 1 – 17.

Hug ,Z., and J. Stole.(1998). 'Total Quality Management Contrasts in Manufacturing and Service Industries' *International Journal of quality and Reliability Management* Vol.12,No.9. pp.210-220

IBM (2005), 'The Customer Centric Store', *IBM Business Institute for Business Value Executive Brief.* U. S. A., NY, July.

Icfai University Press (2007), *Customer Centric Business Model: An Introduction.* Available at: www.icfaiuniversitypress.org/books/customer-centricbusiness-ovw.asp (accessed: August 28, 2007).

Increasing Productivity. (2005). *Employee Network Monitoring.* Available at: www.employee-netwok-moniering.com (Accessed: August 11,2006).

J. Kirkby, J. Wecksell, et al., ed (2003) 'The value of customer experience management'. *Strategic Analysis Report,* Gartner Inc.

Jack W. Wiley, Scott M. Brooks, and Kyle M. Lundby (2006), 'Put Your Employees on the Other Side of the Microscope,' *Human Resource Planning* 29.2.

Jackson, D. Jr. (1994) 'Relationship selling: the personalization of relationship marketing', *Asia-Australia Marketing Journal,* August, pp. 45-54.

James Peltier, John A.schibrowsky, Done E. Schultz, and Debra Zahay (2006) 'Interactive IMC: The Relational- Transactional Continuum and the Synergistic Use of Customer Data,' *Journal of Advertising Research,* Vol. 42, No.2.

Jay R. Galbraith (2005), *Designing the Customer Centric Organization,* San Francisco: Jossey Bass

Jim Mclennan, Olga Pavlou and Mary M. Omodei,(2005) 'Chapter 14 Cognitive Control Processes Discriminate Between Better versus Poorer Performance by Fire Ground Commanders, How Professionals Make Decisions', in Henry Montgomery, Raanan Lipshitz and Berndt Berhmer (ed.) *How Professionals Make Decisions*. Mahwah, NJ: Lawrence Associates, p. 210.

John B. Miner (2002), *Organizational Behavior: Foundations, Theories and Analysis*, New York: Oxford University Press, p. 240

http://www.questia.com/PM.qst?a=o&d=108106577 John Beckford, (2002), *Quality*, London: Routledge, p. 60.

John Gray (2006). *Motivating Employees*. John Gray Awards. Available at: www.johngray.com/employeemotivation.aspx (Accessed August 20, 2007).

John H. Harris, and Lucy A. Arendt (1998), 'Stress Reduction and the Small Business: Increasing Employee and Customer Satisfaction,' *SAM Advanced Management Journal* 63.1.

John Petter, Patricia Byrnes, Do-Lim Choi, Frank Fegan and Randy Miller (2002) 'Dimentions and Patterns in Employee Empowerment: Assessing What Matters to Street-level Bureaucrats,' *Journal of Public Administration Research and Theory*, Vol. 12, No. 3.

John W. Newstorm (2002) 'Making Work Fun: An Important role for Managers,' *SAM Advanced Management Journal*, Vol. 67 No.1

Klein, Hal. (1999. "Customer Service Strategies."Computer Associates, White Paper.

Lauren Beilski (2005) 'Razor Sharp ROI Calculations: Yes, It's Possible to Get a Perspective on IT Value, but You Have to Do the Measurement Right' *ABA Banking Journal*, Vol. 97, No. 10.

Lauren Bielski (2004), 'The Case for Business Process Outsourcing: Yes, You Can Renovate Process and Cut Costs, but Make No Assumptions and Get Specific,' *ABA Banking Journal* 96.5.

Levine, J. (1992) Relationship marketing, *Forbes*, 20 December, pp. 232-4.

Levit, Theodore (1960), 'Marketing Myopia', *Harvard Business Review*, 38, (July-August) 26-44, 173-180.

Lindgreen, A. (2004) 'The design, implementation and monitoring of a CRM programme: a case study', *Marketing Intelligence & Planning*, Volume 22, No. 2, pp. 160-186.

Lindner, James R. (1998). 'Understanding Employee Motivation' *Journal of Extension*, June 1998, Vol.36 No. 3

Lisa H. Nishii, and Benjamin Schneider (2004), 'Chapter 12 HRM in Service the Contingencies Abound,' in Ronald J. Burke and Cary L. Cooper (ed.), Reinventing *Human Resources Management: Challenges and New Directions*, New York: Routledge, p. 225.

Lundin, Stephen C., Christensen, John and Harry Paul.(2002). *Fish Tales.* New York: Hyprion.

MacGregor, Diane (2006). *Internal Communication: it's not Rocket Science!*, Nova Scotia: Crown.

Marc Hanlan (2004), *High Performance Teams: How to Make Them Work*, Westport, CT: Praeger, p 82.

Martha R., Don Peppers (1993) *The One to One Future Building Relationships One Customer at a Time*, New York: Doubleday Group Inc.

Measuring (2006). *Measuring What Matters.* Available at: www.customer-feedback-surveys.net (Accessed: January 7,2007).

Meicevole, Sintitia (2006) *Characteristics of a Successful Entrepreneur.* Article to Go. Available at : http://www.articletogo.com (Accessed: August 13, 2007).

Michael H., James C. (1993) *Reengineering Corporation*, New York: Doubleday Inc.

Michael J. Albers (2005) *Communication of Complex Information: User Goals and Information Needs for Dynamic Web Information*, Mahwash, NJ: Lawrence Erlbaum Assosiates, pp.68 -109

Michael K. Hui, Kevin Au, and Henry Fock (2004), 'Empowerment Effects across Cultures,' *Journal of International Business Studies* 35.1.

Michael Rohloff (1997), *Business Process Modelling Springer. An object Oriented Approach.*

Mintzberg H. (1989), *Mintzberg Management – Inside our Strange World of Organziations:*, U. S. A.: Macmillian Inc.

Misha W. Vaughan, and Joseph S. Dumas (2005), *27 Web-Based Programs and Applications for Business*, in Robert W. Proctor and Kim-Phuong L. Vu (ed.) Handbook of Human Factors in Web Design. Mahwah, NJ: Lawrence Erlbaum Associates, pp. 497- 499.

Molineus, P. (2002) *Exploiting CRM: Connecting With Customers*, London: Hodder & Stoughton.

Morley,M.,and N.Heraty (1995). 'The high Performance Organization: Developing Teamwork where it Counts.' *Management Decision*, Vol.33, No. 2., pp 56-64.

Nelson, S. D (2003). *Management Update: The Eight Building Blocks of CRM.* Available at: Gartner,*www2.cio.com/analyst/report1483.html* , (Accessed : 19/6/2007).

Newman D. (1973), *Organization Design and Analytical Approach to Structuring of organizations*, London: Edward Arnold Ltd.

Olaf Zuknft and Frank Rump (2000), *'Business Process Modeling Springer From Business Process Modeling to Workflow Management: An Integrated Approach'.*

Oliva, Regelio and John D. Sterman (2001), 'Cutting Corners and Working Overtime: Quality Erosion in the Service Industry', *Management Journal of Marketing*, Vol. 47, pp. 894 – 914.

Olve, N-G., Roy, J., Wetter, M. (2000) *Performance Drivers: A Practical Guide to Using the Balanced Scorecard*, Chichester: Wiley.

Oslon E. M., Slater S. F. and Hult T. M. (2005) 'The Performance Implications of Fit Among Business Strategies, Marketing Organization Structure and Strategic Behaviour', *Journal of Marketing*, Vol. 69, No. 3, pp. 49-65.

Pat Auger (2005) 'The Impact of Interactivity and Design Sophistication on the Performance of Commercial Web Sites for Small Businesses', *Journal of Small Business Management*, Vol. 43, No. 2.

Payne, Andrian and Pennie Frow (2005), 'A strategic Frame Work for Customer Relationship Management', *Journal of Marketing*, Vol. 69, No. 4, pp. 167–176.

Pepotone, James (2006). 'Knowledge Leadership: Job Satisfaction', *Peptone worldwide.*

Philip J. Kitchen, and Patrick De Pelsmacker (2004) *Integrated Marketing Communications A Printer*, New York: Routledge, p. 48.

Ponsonby, R. (2004), 'Customer Relationship Management – The Importance of Market Segmentation and Appropriate Measurement', *IBM Global Services.*

Ranjay and James (2005) 'The Quest for Customer Focus', *Harvard Business Review.* Aug. 21, Vol.18, No. 6

Ranjit Bose R. (2002), Customer Relation Management: Key Components for IT Success, *Industrial Management and And Data Systems,* Vol. 102 No. 2, pp. 89–97.

Rampersad, H.K., Authentic Personal Brand Coaching; Entrepreneurial Leadership Brand Coaching for Sustainable High Performance. Information Age Publishing, USA, 2015.

Rampersad, H.K. Authentic Governance; Aligning Personal Governance with Corporate Governance, Springer USA, New York, 2014

Rampersad, H.K., Authentic Personal Branding: A new blueprint for building and aligning a powerful leadership brand, Information Age Publishing, USA, 2009; Pearson Malaysia, 2008.

Rampersad, H.K., The Personal Balanced Scorecard; The Way to Individual Happiness, Personal Integrity and Organizational Effectiveness, Information Age Publishing, USA, 2006.

Rampersad, H.K., Total Performance Scorecard; Redefining Management to Achieve Performance with Integrity, Elsevier Science, USA, 2003

Raul Katz, Paul Kocourek, Decui Mends and Gray Niclson (2004), 'Telecommunication Service Providers: A New Model Operating', *Booz Allen Hamilton Inc.,* pp. 1 -10.

Reche, Bill. (2006). "Why some Employee Recognition Programs Backfire. ." Top Result.com. Available at: www.topresults.com/creating_an_effective_Employee.usp. (Accessed: August 3.2007).

Reichheld, F. F., Sasser, W. E. Jr. (1990) 'Zero Defections: Quality Comes To Services', *Harvard Business Review*, Volume 68, No. 5, pp. 105–111.

Reichheld, Frederic F.(1996). *The Loyalty Effect:* The Hidden Force Behind Growth, Profits and Lasting value. Boston: Harvard Business School Press.

Reiger, Tom. (2006). "Engaging Customers—All Day, Everyday." *The Gallup Management Journal,* September 14.

Reinartz, Werner J. and V. Kumar (2000), 'On the Profitability of Long Life Customers in Non Contractual Setting: An Empirical Investigation and Implications for Marketing', *Journal of Marketing*, Vol. 64, pp.17-35.

Reinartz, Werner J., Manfred Krafft, and Wayne D. Hoyer (2004) 'The CRM process: Its Measurement and Impact on Performance', *Journal of Marketing Research*, pp. 293-305.

Richard P. Bagozzi, and Utpal M. Dohalakia, (2004) 'Chapter 2 'Three Roles of Past Experience in Goal Setting and Goal Triving, ', in Timann Betsch and Susanne Haberstoh (ed.) *The Routines of Decision Making* Mahwah, NJ; Lawrence Erlbaum Associates, p. 22.

Robert Angle (2004), 'Sustaining Profitable Customer Relationships Requires Real Leadership', *Ivey Business Journal online*, pp. 1-7.

Robert J.Thierauf (2001) *Effective Business Intelligence Systems*, Westport, CT: Quorum Books, p.280.

Rodwell, J.J., Kienzie. R. and M.A Shadur (1998). 'The Relationship Among Work Related Participations, Employees Attitudes, and Employee Performance: The Integral role of Communication.' *Human resource Management*, Vol. 37. No. (3&4). pp.277-293.

Rohbacher, Blake. (2001). "The Elements of Good Online Service." *E-Commerce Guide*, September 26, 2001 Ed.

Ron Rosenberg (2006), 'Getting to the Heart of Customer Satisfaction: How to Make Your Business Customer Centric.', *Rural Telecommunication Journal*, July, 2006, Volume. 25, No. 4.

Ross, J.E.(1999). *Total Quality Management Text, Cases and Reading* .3rd ed.pp.23-25.

Rust Roland T., Tim Ambler, Gregory S. Carpenter, U Kumar and Rajendra K. Srivastua (2002), 'Measuring Marketing Productivity: Current Knowledge and Future Directions', *Journal of Marketing*, Vol. 64, pp. 17-35.

S. Ratneshwar, David Glen Mick, and Cynthia Huffman, eds., (2000) *The Why of Consumption: Contemporary Perspective on Customer Motives, Goals and Desires*, London: Routledge, p. 11.

Sarah Cook (2002), *Customer Care Excellence: How to Create an Effective Customer FocusUSA:* Kogan Page Limited.

Saxby, avid. (2006). "If you aren't Measuring Customer Service, You aren't managing It."Measure-X White Paper.

Scheuing E. E. (1999), 'Achieving Excellence – Creating Customer Passion', *Hospital Material Management Quarterly*, Vol. 21, No. 1.

Scott, J.L. (2001). 'Customer service: Accept Responsibility for Fixing Errors.' *Frugal marketing article*. Available at: www.frugalmarketing.com. (Accessed: March 11, 2007)

Selland, Jennifer. (2006). "Delivering Great Customer Service." *Customer Service Magazine*. Available at: www.customervicemanager.com (Accessed: December 30, 2006.)Senge, Peter M. (1990). *The fifth Discipline: The Art& Practice of the learning organization* .Nawyork: Doubleday, 1990.

Senge, Peter.M. (1990). *The Fifth Discipline the Art Practice of the learning Organization* New York: Doubleday.

Show, C. (2005) *Revolutionize your Customer Experience*. New York: Palgrave Macmillan.

Sirota, David.Mi schkind, Louis and Michael Irwin Meltzer. (2005) 'The Enthusiastic Employee. Upper saddle River': *Pearson Education, Inc.*

Slagle, Richard (2006*). Communication: The Essential Workplace Skill.* County Magazine. Available at: www.county.org/resources/library/county_mag/county/132comm.html (Accessed:August 3.2007).

Special reports. (2006) 'Managing Teamwork', *National Business Research Institute, Inc.*

Srivastavam Rajendea K., Tasaddug A. Shervani and Liam Fahey (1998), 'Market Base Assets and Shore Holder Value: A Frame Work for Analysis', *Journal of Marketing*, Vol. 62, pp. 55–66.

Stein, Steven J. and Howard E. Book (2000) The EQ Edge, New York: Stoddard Publishing Company Limited

Subhash C. Kundu, and Jay A. Vora (2004), 'Creating a Talented Workforce for Delivering Service Quality', *Human Resource Planning* 27.2.

Suzanne Dibble (1999), *Keeping Your Valuable Employees: Retention Strategies for Your Organization's Most Important Resource*, New York: John Wiley & Sons, p 89.

Sveiby, K. E. (1996) *The New Organizational Wealth.* San Francisco, CA: Berret-Koehler.

Theodore L. (1960) 'Marketing Myopia', *Harvard Business Review*, Vol. 16, No.8.

Theresa K. Lant and Zur Shapir, eds., (2001) *Organizational Cognition: Computation and Interpretation*, Mahwah, NJ: Lawrence Erlbaum Associates, pp. 52–53.

The Sergay Group, 2014, http://www.sergaygroup.com/Smart-Talk/Strategic-Alignment.html

Varelas, Elaine. (2005) 'Communicating in your Culture: "What are you Really Saying to Employees?' *Boston works, article.* October 3.

Wellins, Richard Byham William and Jeanne M. Wilson (1991) *Empowered Teams): Creating self-Directed Work Group that Improve Quality, Productivity, and Participation*, San Francisco .Jossey-Bass.

Wheelihan, Kathleen. (2002). 'Sweat the Small Stuff for Great Customer Service.' AchieveMax Consulting, White Paper.

Wilkins A.L (1989).*Developing corporate character*, San Francisco: Jossey-Bass.

Wilson, J. (1997) *Varieties of Police Behavior*, Cambridge: Harvard University Press.

Yenkatesan, Rajkumar and V. Kumar (2004), 'A Customer Lifetime Value Framework for Analysis', *Journal of Marketing*, Vol. 62, pp. 55–66.

Zablah, Alex R., Danny N. Bellenger, and Wesley J. Johnston (2004) 'Customer Relationship Management Implementation Gaps', *Journal of Personal Selling and Sales Management*, pp. 279-95.

Zairi M. (1999), 'Managing Customer Satisfaction: a Best Practice Perspective', *The TQM Magazine*, Vol. 12 No. 6.

Zemke, Ron. (2003).*Delivering Knock Your Socks off Service.*New York: American Management Association.

About the Author

Dr. Saad Bin Dhafer Al-Qahtani holds a Doctorate Degree in Business Administration from Nottingham University, an MBA from KSU, and a Bachelor of Engineering from KFUPM. He is a versatile executive leader with an impeccable execution track record in communications, technology and media eco-system with distinguishing awards and honors over a 25 years of experience. As former CEO of Strategic Operations, VP of Home Business Unit and GM of Corporate Communications at the STC, the largest integrated telecommunications operator in KSA with a market capitalization of 110+ billion riyal, he was instrumental in solidifying capabilities across human capital, regulatory readiness, customer experience quality, broadband network roll-out program, and agile program management. Dr. Saad was also instrumental in growing broadband penetration from single digits to 50+% levels every year and a key catalyst in introducing the IP based TV and multimedia solutions for the first time in KSA. He was also the originator in launching a loyalty and rewards biggest program in ME called Qitaf. He was also involved in enabling STC to move into adjacent multibillion dollar IT solutions markets timely and swiftly. He was also the key catalyst in outsourcing programs for cost efficiency and operational excellence at STC.

Authentic Customer Centricity, pages 103–104
Copyright © 2015 by Information Age Publishing
All rights of reproduction in any form reserved.

As an active board member at Gulf Allied Digital Media (Intigral), he played an important role in introducing a revamping content play for STC and the KSA region, which became a key ingredient success factor for IP based TV and media solutions. As an active board member in Turk Telekom (Avea), the largest telecom operator in Turkey, he influenced the company to enter into ICT eco-system and influenced the largest fiber infrastructure buy out in Europe. This was a huge catalyst influencing the company offering first convergence products in Turkey. He is well known for his successful business executions, innovative leadership skills, delivering sustainable value, and increasing broadband penetration by double digit growths year over year. Dr. Saad received prestigious awards and honors, such as "Best Marketing GM Award" by "The Arabian Business Achievement Awards 2005" and the "Arabian Bizz Award 2009," the highest award granted by the World Confederation of Business. He can be reached at sdhafer@kadidigital.com and www.kadidigital.com

Printed in the United States
By Bookmasters